CULTURE AND ANARCHY

BY

MATTHEW ARNOLD

Prophets of Sensibility:
Precursors of Modern Cultural Thought

GENERAL EDITOR
PROFESSOR HAROLD BLOOM
YALE UNIVERSITY

CHELSEA HOUSE
NEW YORK 1983

This edition is an edited reprint of the 1949 edition
by The Viking Press
Copyright © 1983 by Chelsea House Publishers
All rights reserved
Printed and bound in the United States of America

ISBN: 0-87754-329-1

PROPHETS OF SENSIBILITY: PRECURSORS OF MODERN CULTURAL THOUGHT

by Harold Bloom
Professor of the Humanities
Yale University

It was one of the peculiarities of literary Modernism, in the Age of Pound, Joyce and Eliot, and of their New Critical followers, to argue that the imaginative literature of the twentieth century had its true origins in seventeenth-century sensibility. In this polemical contention, Eliot could insist that his poetic and critical stance, or more simply his personal culture, had its sources in Lancelot Andrewes and John Donne, rather, say, than in Walter Pater and Matthew Arnold. Assertions of a remote ancestry have the special charm of escaping the immediate squalors of the family romance. We need not smile too ironically at the personal mythologies of an Eliot or a Pound when we reflect upon the even more formidable Sigmund Freud, who in *Beyond the Pleasure Principle* cheerfully proclaims his descent from Empedocles, safely distant at two millennia, while stubbornly denying his palpable precursor, Arthur Schopenhauer.

But the wry humor of these necessary strategems of the spirit cannot be allowed to obscure the truth of intellectual and aesthetic genealogy. Wallace Stevens once remarked that genealogy is the art of correcting other genealogists' mistakes. One broad way of characterizing the Prophets of Sensibility series is to observe that it intends to correct Eliot's persuasive misreading of the family relationship between nineteenth- and twentieth-century thought and literature. A book like Walter Pater's early masterpiece, *The Renaissance,* reverberates endlessly in such characteristic modern creators as Yeats, Eliot, Joyce, Pound, Stevens, Woolf, Hart Crane, and even in a vitalistic heretic like D. H. Lawrence. None of them (except for Yeats) would have granted Pater's authority and fatherhood, yet he haunts them all (and many others) both in cadence and in concept. Pater, like Arnold, Ruskin, Carlyle, Butler, Hazlitt, De Quincey, and Coleridge is simply too close for the comfort of autonomy to assert itself.

Certainly the anxiety of influence is a crucial sorrow in the vexed story of the true heritage of Modernism. But, as an anxiety, it may conceal deeper continuities between Romantic and Victorian forerunners and their belated heirs. Prophecy, an ancient Hebraic mode of literature, became in the nineteenth century a new kind of vitalistic mode, one that erased the always wavering boundaries between criticism and creation. What, after all, is the literary genre of Pater's *The Renaissance?* The prose *Imaginary Conversations* of Landor and the verse monologues of Browning are no more radical as experiments than are these reveries of Walter Pater. Pater blends moral reflection, prose poetry, psychological portraiture, art and literary criticism, cultural history and a curious kind of mythopoeic fiction into an amalgam that defies conventional description, but that has the ultimate purpose of subverting Christian evaluations of the *agon* between the desires of this world and the work of the spirit. As a prophet, Pater restores to art the epiphanies appropriated by orthodox dualisms, whether of religion or of philosophy.

Pater's *The Renaissance* dramatizes the authentic burden of the Prophets of Sensibility. This burden is not so much secularization as it is the problematic transferences and descents of authority from earlier times, when it could be recognized and accepted, to the threshold of our age, where authority can be recognized precisely as what has vanished, and what could not be accepted if somehow it reappeared. Freud, who devised the clinical transference of the model of the taboo, attempted to make of psychoanalysis a modernist *praxis* that would reestablish the images of authority upon a supposedly scientific basis. Ruskin, Carlyle, Pater and the other Victorian prophets assumed, rather, that authority could be established again only upon an aesthetic basis. Had Freud (and Nietzsche) written in English, we would group them now with the Prophets of Sensibility. Science and philosophy, like religion, have yielded to the literary culture, and the pragmatic consequences of that yielding are at the center of Romantic and Victorian prophecy.

Prophecy, in the Hebraic sense, was moral truth-telling of the most violent kind, always following the formula of "The Word of God came to me . . ." The God Word that came to the nineteenth-century prophets mixed perception and sensation into a new kind of sensibility, one that is still with us today. Difficult to describe, this sensibility emphasizes a continuum haunted by intimations of mortality punctuated by brief bursts of radiance–privileged moments in which a peculiar vividness gives the illusion of redeeming life. It may be the stigma of the nineteenth-century Prophets of Sensibility that (except for Pater) they sought to combat this climate of the spirit but oddly fostered it implicitly (even as Pater did so overtly). The increasing internalization of the self depended upon an augmentation of estrangement from the object world, and what was intended as prophetic warning and lament as to this estrangement became instead a subtle suggestion of an inevitable movement in elite sensibility.

Today we have the strange anomaly that Nietzsche, the Continental version of the Prophets of Sensibility, is credited with fathering the future, while the

Prophets are neglected. But time's revenges work themselves out, and these writers will father the future again, even as they prophesied our current sensibility. They could not save or even preserve the post-Christian spirituality they sought to imbue in society, but they fostered in its place a pragmatic triumph of literary culture, beyond religion and beyond speculative philosophy. Psychoanalysis, despite its scientism, is only another form of that literary culture. So, in another way, are the textualist literary criticism and language-oriented "human sciences" that are vivid parts of Structuralist and post-Structuralist formulations. There are true and false prophets of sensibility, even as there were true and false prophets among the ancient Hebrews. The test for prophecy finally is canonization; the books that return from the dead certify themselves as inescapable, and so as a vital part of the truth. We can say of each of us in relation to the books in this Prophets of Sensibility series what Pater said of his hero in *Marius the Epicurean*. The experience of reading them

> . . . gave him a definitely ascertained measure of his moral or intellectual need, of the demand his soul must make upon the powers, whatsoever they might be, which had brought him, as he was, into the world at all. . . .

CULTURE AND ANARCHY

○

I N ONE of his speeches a short time ago, that fine
speaker and famous Liberal, Mr. Bright, took occasion to have a fling at the friends and preachers of culture. "People who talk about what they call *culture*!"
said he, contemptuously; "by which they mean a smattering of the two dead languages of Greek and Latin."
And he went on to remark, in a strain with which modern speakers and writers have made us very familiar,
how poor a thing this culture is, how little good it can do
to the world, and how absurd it is for its possessors to set
much store by it. And the other day a younger Liberal
than Mr. Bright, one of a school whose mission it is to
bring into order and system that body of truth with
which the earlier Liberals merely fumbled, a member of
the University of Oxford, and a very clever writer, Mr.
Frederic Harrison, developed, in the systematic and
stringent manner of his school, the thesis which Mr.
Bright had propounded in only general terms. "Perhaps
the very silliest cant of the day," said Mr. Frederic Harrison, "is the cant about culture. Culture is a desirable

1

quality in a critic of new books, and sits well on a possessor of *belles lettres*; but as applied to politics, it means simply a turn for small fault-finding, love of selfish ease, and indecision in action. The man of culture is in politics one of the poorest mortals alive. For simple pedantry and want of good sense no man is his equal. No assumption is too unreal, no end is too unpractical for him. But the active exercise of politics requires common sense, sympathy, trust, resolution, and enthusiasm, qualities which your man of culture has carefully rooted up, lest they damage the delicacy of his critical olfactories. Perhaps they are the only class of responsible beings in the community who cannot with safety be entrusted with power."

Now for my part I do not wish to see men of culture asking to be entrusted with power; and, indeed, I have freely said, that in my opinion the speech most proper, at present, for a man of culture to make to a body of his fellow-countrymen who get him into a committee-room, is Socrates's: *Know thyself!* and this is not a speech to be made by men wanting to be entrusted with power. For this very indifference to direct political action I have been taken to task by the *Daily Telegraph*, coupled, by a strange perversity of fate, with just that very one of the Hebrew prophets whose style I admire the least, and called "an elegant Jeremiah." It is because I say (to use the words which the *Daily Telegraph* puts in my mouth) :—"You mustn't make a fuss because you have no vote,—that is vulgarity; you mustn't hold big meetings to agitate for reform bills and to repeal corn laws,—that is the very height of vulgarity,"—it is for this reason that I am called sometimes an elegant Jere miah, sometimes a spurious Jeremiah, a Jeremiah abov. the reality of whose mission the writer in the *Daily Telegraph* has his doubts. It is evident, therefore, that I have so taken my line as not to be exposed to the whole brunt of Mr. Frederic Harrison's censure. Still, I have often spoken in praise of culture, I have striven to make all my works and ways serve the interests of culture. I take culture to be something a great deal more than what Mr. Frederic Harrison and others call it: "a desirable quality in a critic of new books." Nay, even though to a certain extent I am disposed to agree with Mr. Frederic Harrison, that men of culture are just the class of responsible beings in this community of ours who cannot properly, at present, be entrusted with power, I am not sure that I do not think this the fault of our community rather than of the men of culture. In short, although, like Mr. Bright and Mr. Frederic Harrison, and the editor of the *Daily Telegraph,* and a large body of valued friends of mine, I am a Liberal, yet I am a Liberal tempered by experience, reflection, and renouncement, and I am, above all, a believer in culture. Therefore I propose now to try and inquire, in the simple unsystematic way which best suits both my taste and my powers, what culture really is, what good it can do, what is our own special need of it; and I shall seek to find some plain grounds on which a faith in culture,—both my own faith in it and the faith of others,—may rest securely.

I. SWEETNESS AND LIGHT

The disparagers of culture make its motive curiosity; sometimes, indeed, they make its motive mere exclusiveness and vanity. The culture which is supposed to plume itself on a smattering of Greek and Latin is a culture which is begotten by nothing so intellectual as curiosity; it is valued either out of sheer vanity and ignorance or else as an engine of social and class distinction, separating its holder, like a badge or title, from other people who have not got it. No serious man would call this *culture*, or attach any value to it, as culture, at all. To find the real ground for the very different estimate which serious .people will set upon culture, we must find some motive for culture in the terms of which may lie a real ambiguity; and such a motive the word *curiosity* gives us.

I have before now pointed out that we English do not, like the foreigners, use this word in a good sense as well as in a bad sense. With us the word is always used in a somewhat disapproving sense. A liberal and intelligent eagerness about the things of the mind may be meant by a foreigner when he speaks of curiosity, but with us the word always conveys a certain notion of frivolous and unedifying activity. In the *Quarterly Review,* some little time ago, was an estimate of the celebrated French critic, M. Sainte-Beuve, and a very inadequate estimate it in my judgment was. And its inadequacy consisted chiefly in this: that in our English way it left out of sight the double sense really involved in the word *curiosity,* thinking enough was said to stamp M. Sainte-Beuve with blame if it was said that he was impelled in his operations as a critic by curiosity, and omitting either to perceive that M. Sainte-Beuve himself, and many other people with him, would consider that this was praiseworthy and not blameworthy, or to point out why it ought really to be accounted worthy of blame and not of praise. For as there is a curiosity about intellectual matters which is futile, and merely a disease, so there is certainly a curiosity,—a desire after the things of the mind simply for their own sakes and for the pleasure of seeing them as they are,—which is, in an intelligent being, natural and laudable. Nay, and the very desire to see things as they are implies a balance and regulation of mind which is not often attained without fruitful effort, and which is the very opposite of the blind and diseased impulse of mind which is what we mean to blame when we blame curiosity. Montesquieu says: "The first motive which ought to impel us to study is the desire to augment the excellence of our nature, and to render an intelligent being yet more intelligent." This is the true ground to assign for the genuine scientific passion, however manifested, and for culture, viewed simply as a fruit of this passion; and it is a worthy ground, even though we let the term *curiosity* stand to describe it.

But there is of culture another view, in which not solely the scientific passion, the sheer desire to see things as they are, natural and proper in an intelligent being, appears as the ground of it. There is a view in which all the love of our neighbour, the impulses towards action, help, and beneficence, the desire for removing human error, clearing human confusion, and diminishing human misery, the noble aspiration to leave the world better and happier than we found it,—motives eminently such as are called social,—come in as part of the grounds of culture, and the main and pre-eminent part. Culture is then properly described not as having its origin in curiosity, but as having its origin in the love of perfection; it is *a study of perfection*. It moves by the force, not merely or primarily of the scientific passion for pure knowledge, but also of the moral and social passion for doing good. As, in the first view of it, we took for its worthy motto Montesquieu's words: "To render an intelligent being yet more intelligent!" so, in the second view of it, there is no better motto which it can have than these words of Bishop Wilson: "To make reason and the will of God prevail!"

Only, whereas the passion for doing good is apt to

be overhasty in determining what reason and the will
of God say, because its turn is for acting rather than
thinking and it wants to be beginning to act; and whereas
it is apt to take its own conceptions, which proceed from
its own state of development and share in all the imper-
fections and immaturities of this, for a basis of action;
what distinguishes culture is, that it is possessed by the
scientific passion as well as by the passion of doing good;
that it demands worthy notions of reason and the will
of God, and does not readily suffer its own crude conceptions to substitute themselves for them. And knowing
that no action or institution can be salutary and stable
which is not based on reason and the will of God, it is
not so bent on acting and instituting, even with the
great aim of diminishing human error and misery ever
before its thoughts, but that it can remember that acting
and instituting are of little use, unless we know how and
what we ought to act and to institute.

This culture is more interesting and more far-reaching
than that other, which is founded solely on the scientific
passion for knowing. But it needs times of faith and
ardour, times when the intellectual horizon is opening
and widening all round us, to flourish in. And is not the
close and bounded intellectual horizon within which we
have long lived and moved now lifting up, and are not
new lights finding free passage to shine in upon us? For
a long time there was no passage for them to make their
way in upon us, and then it was of no use to think of
adapting the world's action to them. Where was the
hope of making reason and the will of God prevail
among people who had a routine which they had chris-
tened reason and the will of God, in which they were
inextricably bound, and beyond which they had no
power of looking? But now the iron force of adhesion

to the old routine,—social, political, religious,—has wonderfully yielded; the iron force of exclusion of all which is new has wonderfully yielded. The danger now is, not that people should obstinately refuse to allow anything but their old routine to pass for reason and the will of God, but either that they should allow some novelty or other to pass for these too easily, or else that they should underrate the importance of them altogether, and think it enough to follow action for its own sake, without troubling themselves to make reason and the will of God prevail therein. Now, then, is the moment for culture to be of service, culture which believes in making reason and the will of God prevail, believes in perfection, is the study and pursuit of perfection, and is no longer debarred, by a rigid invincible exclusion of whatever is new, from getting acceptance for its ideas, simply because they are new.

The moment this view of culture is seized, the moment it is regarded not solely as the. endeavour to see things as they are, to draw towards a knowledge of the universal order which seems to be intended and aimed at in the world, and which it is a man's happiness to go along with or his misery to go counter to,—to learn, in short, the will of God,—the moment, I say, culture is considered not merely as the endeavour to *see* and *learn* this, but as the endeavour, also, to make it *prevail*, the moral, social, and beneficent character of culture becomes manifest. The mere endeavour to see and learn the truth for our own personal satisfaction is indeed a commencement for making it prevail, a preparing the way for this, which always serves this, and is wrongly, therefore, stamped with blame absolutely in itself and not only in its caricature and degeneration. But perhaps it has got stamped with blame, and disparaged with tho dubious title of curiosity, because in comparison with this wider endeavour of such great and plain utility it looks selfish, petty, and unprofitable.

And religion, the greatest and most important of the efforts by which the human race has manifested its impulse to perfect itself,—religion, that voice of the deepest human experience,—does not only enjoin and sanction the aim which is the great aim of culture, the aim of setting ourselves to ascertain what perfection is and to make it prevail; but also, in determining generally in what human perfection consists, religion comes to a conclusion identical with that which culture,—culture seeking the determination of this question through *all* the voices of human experience which have been heard upon it, of art, science, poetry, philosophy, history, as well as of religion, in order to give a greater fulness and certainty to its solution,—likewise reaches. Religion says: *The kingdom of God is within you;* and culture, in like manner, places human perfection in an *internal* condition, in the growth and predominance of our humanity proper, as distinguished from our animality. It places it in the ever-increasing efficacy and in the general harmonious expansion of those gifts of thought and feeling, which make the peculiar dignity, wealth, and happiness of human nature. As I have said on a former occasion: "It is in making endless additions to itself, in the endless expansion of its powers, in endless growth in wisdom and beauty, that the spirit of the human race finds its ideal. To reach this ideal, culture is an indispensable aid, and that is the true value of culture." Not a having and a resting, but a growing and a becoming, is the character of perfection as culture conceives it; and here, too, it coincides with religion.

And because men are all members of one great whole, and the sympathy which is in human nature will not allow one member to be indifferent to the rest or to have a perfect welfare independent of the rest, the expansion of our humanity, to suit the idea of perfection which culture forms, must be a *general* expansion. Perfection, as culture conceives it, is not possible while the individual remains isolated. The individual is required, under pain of being stunted and enfeebled in his own development if he disobeys, to carry others along with him in his march towards perfection, to be continually doing all he can to enlarge and increase the volume of the human stream sweeping thitherward. And here, once more, culture lays on us the same obligation as religion, which says, as Bishop Wilson has admirably put it, that "to promote the kingdom of God is to increase and hasten one's own happiness."

But, finally, perfection,—as culture from a thorough disinterested study of human nature and human experience learns to conceive it,—is a harmonious expansion of *all* the powers which make the beauty and worth of human nature, and is not consistent with the over-development of any one power at the expense of the rest. Here culture goes beyond religion, as religion is generally conceived by us.

If culture, then, is a study of perfection, and of harmonious perfection, general perfection, and perfection which consists in becoming something rather than in having something, in an inward condition of the mind and spirit, not in an outward set of circumstances,—it is clear that culture, instead of being the frivolous and useless thing which Mr. Bright, and Mr. Frederic Harrison, and many other Liberals are apt to call it, has a very important function to fulfil for mankind. And this function is particularly important in our modern world, of which the whole civilisation is, to a much greater degree than the civilisation of Greece and Rome, mechanical and external, and tends constantly to become more so. But above all in our own country has culture a weighty part to perform, because here that mechanical character, which civilisation tends to take everywhere, is shown in the most eminent degree. Indeed nearly all the characters of perfection, as culture teaches us to fix them, meet in this country with some powerful tendency which thwarts them and sets them at defiance. The idea of perfection as an *inward* condition of the mind and spirit is at variance with the mechanical and material civilisation in esteem with us, and nowhere, as I have said, so much in esteem as with us. The idea of perfection as a *general* expansion of the human family is at variance with our strong individualism, our hatred of all limits to the unrestrained swing of the individual's personality, our maxim of "every man for himself." Above all, the idea of perfection as a *harmonious* expansion of human nature is at variance with our want of flexibility, with our inaptitude for seeing more than one side of a thing, with our intense energetic absorption in the particular pursuit we happen to be following. So culture has a rough task to achieve in this country. Its preachers have, and are likely long to have, a hard time of it, and they will much oftener be regarded, for a great while to come, as elegant or spurious Jeremiahs than as friends and benefactors. That, however, will not prevent their doing in the end good service if they persevere. And, meanwhile, the mode of action they have to pursue, and the sort of habits they must fight against, ought to be made quite clear for every one to see, who may be willing to look at the matter attentively and dispassionately.

Faith in machinery is, I said, our besetting danger; often in machinery most absurdly disproportioned to the end which the machinery, if it is to do any good at all, is to serve; but always in machinery, as if it had a value in and for itself. What is freedom but machinery? what is population but machinery? what is coal but machinery? what are railroads but machinery? what is wealth but machinery? what are, even, religious organisations but machinery? Now almost every voice in England is accustomed to speak of these things as if they were precious ends in themselves, and therefore had some of the characters of perfection indisputably joined to them. I have before now noticed Mr. Roebuck's stock argument for proving the greatness and happiness of England as she is, and for quite stopping the mouths of all gainsayers. Mr. Roebuck is never weary of reiterating this argument of his, so I do not know why I should be weary of noticing it. "May not every man in England say what he likes?"—Mr. Roebuck perpetually asks; and that, he thinks, is quite sufficient, and when every man may say what he likes, our aspirations ought to be satisfied. But the aspirations of culture, which is the study of perfection, are not satisfied, unless what men say, when they may say what they like, is worth saying,—has good in it, and more good than bad. In the same way the *Times*, replying to some foreign strictures on the dress, looks, and behaviour of the English abroad, urges that the English ideal is that every one should be free to do and to look just as he likes. But culture indefatigably tries, not to make what each raw person may like the rule by which he fashions himself; but to draw ever nearer to a sense of what is indeed beautiful, graceful, and becoming, and to get the raw person to like that.

And in the same way with respect to railroads and coal. Every one must have observed the strange language current during the late discussions as to the possible failures of our supplies of coal. Our coal, thousands of people were saying, is the real basis of our national greatness; if our coal runs short, there is an end of the greatness of England. But what *is* greatness?—culture makes us ask. Greatness is a spiritual condition worthy to excite love, interest, and admiration; and the outward proof of possessing greatness is that we excite love, interest, and admiration. If England were swallowed up by the sea to-morrow, which of the two, a hundred years hence, would most excite the love, interest, and admiration of mankind,—would most, therefore, show the evidences of having possessed greatness,—the England of the last twenty years, or the England of Elizabeth, of a time of splendid spiritual effort, but when our coal, and our industrial operations depending on coal, were very little developed? Well, then, what an unsound habit of mind it must be which makes us talk of things like coal or iron as constituting the greatness of England, and how salutary a friend is culture, bent on seeing things as they are, and thus dissipating delusions of this kind and fixing standards of perfection that are real!

Wealth, again, that end to which our prodigious works for material advantage are directed,—the commonest of commonplaces tells us how men are always apt to regard wealth as a precious end in itself; and certainly they have never been so apt thus to regard it as they are in England at the present time. Never did people believe anything more firmly than nine Englishmen out of ten at the present day believe that our greatness and welfare are proved by our being so very rich. Now, the use of culture is that it helps us, by means of its spiritual standard of perfection, to regard wealth as but machinery, and not only to say as a matter of words that we regard wealth as but machinery, but really to perceive and feel that it is so. If it were not for this purging effect wrought upon our minds by culture, the whole world, the future as well as the present, would inevitably belong to the

Philistines. The people who believe most that our greatness and welfare are proved by our being very rich, and who most give their lives and thoughts to becoming rich, are just the very people whom we call Philistines. Culture says: "Consider these people, then, their way of life, their habits, their manners, the very tones of their voice; look at them attentively; observe the literature they read, the things which give them pleasure, the words which come forth out of their mouths, the thoughts which make the furniture of their minds; would any amount of wealth be worth having with the condition that one was to become just like these people by having it?" And thus culture begets a dissatisfaction which is of the highest possible value in stemming the common tide of men's thoughts in a wealthy and industrial community, and which saves the future, as one may hope, from being vulgarised, even if it cannot save the present.

Population, again, and bodily health and vigour, are things which are nowhere treated in such an unintelligent, misleading, exaggerated way as in England. Both are really machinery; yet how many people all around us do we see rest in them and fail to look beyond them! Why, one has heard people, fresh from reading certain articles of the *Times* on the Registrar-General's returns of marriages and births in this country, who would talk of our large English families in quite a solemn strain, as if they had something in itself beautiful, elevating, and meritorious in them; as if the British Philistine would have only to present himself before the Great Judge with his twelve children, in order to be received among the sheep as a matter of right!

But bodily health and vigour, it may be said, are not to be classed with wealth and population as mere machinery; they have a more real and essential value. True; but only as they are more intimately connected with a

perfect spiritual condition than wealth or population are.
The moment we disjoin them from the idea of a perfect
spiritual condition, and pursue them, as we do pursue
them, for their own sake and as ends in themselves,
our worship of them becomes as mere worship of machinery, as our worship of wealth or population, and
as unintelligent and vulgarising a worship as that is.
Every one with anything like an adequate idea of human perfection has distinctly marked this subordination
to higher and spiritual ends of the cultivation of bodily
vigour and activity. "Bodily exercise profiteth little; but
godliness is profitable unto all things," says the author
of the Epistle to Timothy. And the utilitarian Franklin
says just as explicitly:—"Eat and drink such an exact
quantity as suits the constitution of thy body, *in refer-
ence to the services of the mind.*" But the point of view
of culture, keeping the mark of human perfection simply
and broadly in view, and not assigning to this perfection,
as religion or utilitarianism assigns to it, a special and
limited character, this point of view, I say, of culture is
best given by these words of Epictetus:—"It is a sign of
ἀφυΐα," says he,—that is, of a nature not finely tempered,
—"to give yourselves up to things which relate to the
body; to make, for instance, a great fuss about exercise,
a great fuss about eating, a great fuss about drinking, a
great fuss about walking, a great fuss about riding. All
these things ought to be done merely by the way: the
formation of the spirit and character must be our real
concern." This is admirable; and, indeed, the Greek
word εὐφυΐα, a finely tempered nature, gives exactly the
notion of perfection as culture brings us to conceive it:
a harmonious perfection, a perfection in which the characters of beauty and intelligence are both present, which
unites "the two noblest of things,"—as Swift, who of one
of the two, at any rate, had himself all too little, most

happily calls them in his *Battle of the Books,*—"the two noblest of things, *sweetness and light.*" The εὐφυής is the man who tends towards sweetness and light; the ἀφυής, on the other hand, is our Philistine. The immense spiritual significance of the Greeks is due to their having been inspired with this central and happy idea of the essential character of human perfection; and Mr. Bright's misconception of culture, as a smattering of Greek and Latin, comes itself, after all, from this wonderful significance of the Greeks having affected the very machinery of our education, and is in itself a kind of homage to it.

In thus makng sweetness and light to be characters of perfection, culture is of like spirit with poetry, follows one law with poetry. Far more than on our freedom, our population, and our industrialism, many amongst us rely upon our religious organisations to save us. I have called religion a yet more important manifestation of human nature than poetry, because it has worked on a broader scale for perfection, and with greater masses of men. But the idea of beauty and of a human nature perfect on all its sides, which is the dominant idea of poetry, is a true and invaluable idea, though it has not yet had the success that the idea of conquering the obvious faults of our animality, and of a human nature perfect on the moral side,—which is the dominant idea of religion,—has been enabled to have; and it is destined, adding to itself the religious idea of a devout energy, to transform and govern the other.

The best art and poetry of the Greeks, in which religion and poetry are one, in which the idea of beauty and of a human nature perfect on all sides adds to itself a religious and devout energy, and works in the strength of that, is on this account of such surpassing interest and instructiveness for us, though it was,—as, having regard to the human race in general, and, indeed, having regard to the Greeks themselves, we must own,—a premature attempt, an attempt which for success needed the moral and religious fibre in humanity to be more braced and developed than it had yet been. But Greece did not err in having the idea of beauty, harmony, and complete human perfection, so present and paramount. It is impossible to have this idea too present and paramount; only, the moral fibre must be braced too. And we, because we have braced the moral fibre, are not on that account in the right way, if at the same time the idea of beauty, harmony, and complete human perfection, is wanting or misapprehended amongst us; and evidently it *is* wanting or misapprehended at present. And when we rely as we do on our religious organisations, which in themselves do not and cannot give us this idea, and think we have done enough if we make them spread and prevail, then, I say, we fall into our common fault of overvaluing machinery.

Nothing is more common than for people to confound the inward peace and satisfaction which follows the subduing of the obvious faults of our animality with what I may call absolute inward peace and satisfaction, —the peace and satisfaction which are reached as we draw near to complete spiritual perfection, and not merely to moral perfection, or rather to relative moral perfection. No people in the world have done more and struggled more to attain this relative moral perfection than our English race has. For no people in the world has the command to *resist the devil, to overcome the wicked one,* in the nearest and most obvious sense of those words, had such a pressing force and reality. And we have had our reward, not only in the great worldly prosperity which our obedience to this command has brought us, but also, and far more, in great inward peace and satisfaction. But to me few things are more pathetic than to see people, on the strength of the inward peace and satisfaction which their rudimentary efforts towards perfection have brought them, employ, concerning their incomplete perfection and the religious organisations within which they have found it, language which properly applies only to complete perfection, and is a far-off echo of the human soul's prophecy of it. Religion itself, I need hardly say, supplies them in abundance with this grand language. And very freely do they use it; yet it is really the severest possible criticism of such an incomplete perfection as alone we have yet reached through our religious organisations.

The impulse of the English race towards moral development and self-conquest has nowhere so powerfully manifested itself as in Puritanism. Nowhere has Puritanism found so adequate an expression as in the religious organisation of the Independents. The modern Independents have a newspaper, the *Nonconformist,* written with great sincerity and ability. The motto, the standard, the profession of faith which this organ of theirs carries aloft, is: "The Dissidence of Dissent and the Protestantism of the Protestant religion." There is sweetness and light, and an ideal of complete harmonious human perfection! One need not go to culture and poetry to find language to judge it. Religion, with its instinct for perfection, supplies language to judge it, language, too, which is in our mouths every day. "Finally, be of one mind, united in feeling," says St. Peter. There is an ideal which judges the Puritan ideal: "The Dissidence of Dissent and the Protestantism of the Protestant religion!" And religious organisations like this are what people believe in, rest in, would give their lives for! Such, I say, is the wonderful virtue of even the beginnings of perfection, of having conquered even the plain faults of our animality, that the religious organisation which has helped us to do it can seem to us something precious, salutary, and to be propagated, even when it wears such a brand of imperfection on its forehead as this. And men have got such a habit of giving to the language of religion a special application, of making it a mere jargon, that for the condemnation which religion itself passes on the shortcomings of their religious organisations they have no ear; they are sure to cheat themselves and to explain this condemnation away. They can only be reached by the criticism which culture, like poetry, speaking a language not to be sophisticated, and resolutely testing these organisations by the ideal of a human perfection complete on all sides, applies to them.

But men of culture and poetry, it will be said, are again and again failing, and failing conspicuously, in the necessary first stage to a harmonious perfection, in the subduing of the great obvious faults of our animality, which it is the glory of these religious organisations to have helped us to subdue. True, they do often so fail. They have often been without the virtues as well as the faults of the Puritan; it has been one of their dangers that they so felt the Puritan's faults that they too much neglected the practice of his virtues. I will not, however, exculpate them at the Puritan's expense. They have often failed in morality, and morality is indispensable. And they have been punished for their failure, as the Puritan has been rewarded for his performance. They have been punished wherein they erred; but their ideal of beauty, of sweetness and light, and a human nature complete on all its sides, remains the true ideal of perfection still; just as the Puritan's ideal of perfection remains narrow and inadequate, although for what he did well he has been richly rewarded. Notwithstanding the mighty results of the Pilgrim Fathers' voyage, they and their standard of perfection are rightly judged when we figure to ourselves Shakespeare or Virgil,—souls in whom sweetness and light, and all that in human nature is most humane, were eminent,—accompanying them on their voyage, and think what intolerable company Shakespeare and Virgil would have found them! In the same way let us judge the religious organisations which we see all around us. Do not let us deny the good and the happiness which they have accomplished; but do not let us fail to see clearly that their idea of human perfection is narrow and inadequate, and that the Dissidence of Dissent and the Protestantism of the Protestant religion will never bring humanity to its true goal. As I said with regard to wealth: Let us look at the life of those who live in and for it,—so I say with regard to the religious organisations. Look at the life imaged in such a newspaper as the *Nonconformist*,—a life of jealousy of the Establishment, disputes, tea-meetings, openings of chapels, sermons; and then think of it as an ideal of a human life completing itself on all sides, and aspiring with all its organs after sweetness, light, and perfection!

Another newspaper, representing, like the *Nonconformist*, one of the religious organisations of this country, was a short time ago giving an account of the crowd at Epsom on the Derby day, and of all the vice and hideousness which was to be seen in that crowd; and then the writer turned suddenly round upon Professor Huxley, and asked him how he proposed to cure all this vice and hideousness without religion. I confess I felt disposed to ask the asker this question: and how do you propose to cure it with such a religion as yours? How is the ideal of a life so unlovely, so unattractive, so incomplete, so narrow, so far removed from a true and satisfying ideal of human perfection, as is the life of your religious organisation as you yourself reflect it, to conquer

and transform all this vice and hideousness? Indeed, the
strongest plea for the study of perfection as pursued by
culture, the clearest proof of the actual inadequacy of
the idea of perfection held by the religious organisations,
—expressing, as I have said, the most widespread effort
which the human race has yet made after perfection,—
is to be found in the state of our life and society with
these in possession of it, and having been in possession
of it I know not how many hundred years. We are all of
us included in some religious organisation or other; we
all call ourselves, in the sublime and aspiring language
of religion which I have before noticed, *children of God.*
Children of God;—it is an immense pretension!—and
how are we to justify it? By the works which we do, and
the words which we speak. And the work which we collective children of God do, our grand centre of life, our
city which we have builded for us to dwell in, is London! London, with its unutterable external hideousness,
and with its internal canker of *publice egestas, privatim
opulentia,*—to use the words which Sallust puts into
Cato's mouth about Rome,—unequalled in the world!
The word, again, which we children of God speak, the
voice which most hits our collective thought, the newspaper with the largest circulation in England, nay, with
the largest circulation in the whole world, is the *Daily
Telegraph!* I say that when our religious organisations,
—which I admit to express the most considerable effort
after perfection that our race has yet made,—land us in
no better result than this, it is high time to examine
carefully their idea of perfection, to see whether it does
not leave out of account sides and forces of human nature which we might turn to great use; whether it would
not be more operative if it were more complete. And I
say that the English reliance on our religious organisations and on their ideas of human perfection just as they

stand, is like our reliance on freedom, on muscular Christianity, on population, on coal, on wealth,—mere belief
in machinery, and unfruitful; and that it is wholesomely
counteracted by culture, bent on seeing things as they
are, and on drawing the human race onwards to a more
complete, a harmonious perfection.

Culture, however, shows its single-minded love of perfection, its desire simply to make reason and the will of
God prevail, its freedom from fanaticism, by its attitude
towards all this machinery, even while it insists that it *is*
machinery. Fanatics, seeing the mischief men do themselves by their blind belief in some machinery or other,
—whether it is wealth and industrialism, or whether
it is the cultivation of bodily strength and activity, or
whether it is a political organisation,—or whether it is
a religious organisation,—oppose with might and main
the tendency to this or that political and religious organisation, or to games and athletic exercises, or to wealth
and industrialism, and try violently to stop it. But the
flexibility which sweetness and light give, and which is
one of the rewards of culture pursued in good faith, enables a man to see that a tendency may be necessary,
and even, as a preparation for something in the future,
salutary, and yet that the generations or individuals who
obey this tendency are sacrificed to it, that they fall
short of the hope of perfection by following it; and that
its mischiefs are to be criticised, lest it should take too
firm a hold and last after it has served its purpose.

Mr. Gladstone well pointed out, in a speech at Paris,
—and others have pointed out the same thing,—how
necessary is the present great movement towards wealth
and industrialism, in order to lay broad foundations of
material well-being for the society of the future. The
worst of these justifications is, that they are generally
addressed to the very people engaged, body and soul, in

the movement in question; at all events, that they are always seized with the greatest avidity by these people, and taken by them as quite justifying their life; and that thus they tend to harden them in their sins. Now, culture admits the necessity of the movement towards fortune-making and exaggerated industrialism, readily allows that the future may derive benefit from it; but insists, at the same time, that the passing generations of industrialists,—forming, for the most part, the stout main body of Philistinism,—are sacrificed to it. In the same way, the result of all the games and sports which occupy the passing generation of boys and young men may be the establishment of a better and sounder physical type for the future to work with. Culture does not set itself against the games and sports; it congratulates the future, and hopes it will make a good use of its improved physical basis; but it points out that our passing generation of boys and young men is, meantime, sacrificed. Puritanism was perhaps necessary to develop the moral fibre of the English race, Nonconformity to break the yoke of ecclesiastical domination over men's minds and to prepare the way for freedom of thought in the distant future; still, culture points out that the harmonious perfection of generations of Puritans and Nonconformists have been, in consequence, sacrificed. Freedom of speech may be necessary for the society of the future, but the young lions of the *Daily Telegraph* in the meanwhile are sacrificed. A voice for every man in his country's government may be necessary for the society of the future, but meanwhile Mr. Beales and Mr. Bradlaugh are sacrificed.

Oxford, the Oxford of the past, has many faults; and she has heavily paid for them in defeat, in isolation, in want of hold upon the modern world. Yet we in Oxford, brought up amidst the beauty and sweetness of that beautiful place, have not failed to seize one truth,—the truth that beauty and sweetness are essential characters of a complete human perfection. When I insist on this, I am all in the faith and tradition of Oxford. I say boldly that this our sentiment for beauty and sweetness, our sentiment against hideousness and rawness, has been at the bottom of our attachment to so many beaten causes, of our opposition to so many triumphant movements. And the sentiment is true, and has never been wholly defeated, and has shown its power even in its defeat. We have not won our political battles, we have not carried our main points, we have not stopped our adversaries' advance, we have not marched victoriously with the modern world; but we have told silently upon the mind of the country, we have prepared currents of feeling which sap our adversaries' position when it seems gained, we have kept up our own communications with the future. Look at the course of the great movement which shook Oxford to its centre some thirty years ago! It was directed, as any one who reads Dr. Newman's *Apology* may see, against what in one word may be called "Liberalism." Liberalism prevailed; it was the appointed force to do the work of the hour; it was necessary, it was inevitable that it should prevail. The Oxford movement was broken, it failed; our wrecks are scattered on every shore:

Quæ regio in terris nostri non plena laboris?

But what was it, this liberalism, as Dr. Newman saw it, and as it really broke the Oxford movement? It was the great middle-class liberalism, which had for the cardinal points of its belief the Reform Bill of 1832, and local self-government, in politics; in the social sphere, free-trade, unrestricted competition, and the making of large industrial fortunes; in the religious sphere, the Dissidence of

Dissent and the Protestantism of the Protestant religion. I do not say that other and more intelligent forces than this were not opposed to the Oxford movement: but this was the force which really beat it; this was the force which Dr. Newman felt himself fighting with; this was the force which till only the other day seemed to be the paramount force in this country, and to be in possession of the future; this was the force whose achievements fill Mr. Lowe with such inexpressible admiration, and whose rule he was so horror-struck to see threatened. And where is this great force of Philistinism now? It is thrust into the second rank, it is become a power of yesterday, it has lost the future. A new power has suddenly appeared, a power which it is impossible yet to judge fully, but which is certainly a wholly different force from middle-class liberalism; different in its cardinal points of belief, different in its tendencies in every sphere. It loves and admires neither the legislation of middle-class Parliaments, nor the local self-government of middle-class vestries, nor the unrestricted competition of middle-class industrialists, nor the dissidence of middle-class Dissent and the Protestantism of middle-class Protestant religion. I am not now praising this new force, or saying that its own ideals are better; all I say is, that they are wholly different. And who will estimate how much the currents of feeling created by Dr. Newman's movements, the keen desire for beauty and sweetness which it nourished, the deep aversion it manifested to the hardness and vulgarity of middle-class liberalism, the strong light it turned on the hideous and grotesque illusions of middle-class Protestantism,—who will estimate how much all these contributed to swell the tide of secret dissatisfaction which has mined the ground under self-confident liberalism of the last thirty years, and has prepared the way for its sudden collapse and supersession? It is in this manner that the sentiment of Oxford for beauty and sweetness conquers, and in this manner long may it continue to conquer!

In this manner it works to the same end as culture, and there is plenty of work for it yet to do. I have said that the new and more democratic force which is now superseding our old middle-class liberalism cannot yet be rightly judged. It has its main tendencies still to form. We hear promises of its giving us administrative reform, law reform, reform of education, and I know not what; but those promises come rather from its advocates, wishing to make a good plea for it and to justify it for superseding middle-class liberalism, than from clear tendencies which it has itself yet developed. But meanwhile it has plenty of well-intentioned friends against whom culture may with advantage continue to uphold steadily its ideal of human perfection; that this is *an inward spiritual activity, having for its characters increased sweetness, increased light, increased life, increased sympathy.* Mr. Bright, who has a foot in both worlds, the world of middle-class liberalism and the world of democracy, but who brings most of his ideas from the world of middle-class liberalism in which he was bred, always inclines to inculcate that faith in machinery to which, as we have seen, Englishmen are so prone, and which has been the bane of middle-class liberalism. He complains with a sorrowful indignation of people who "appear to have no proper estimate of the value of the franchise"; he leads his disciples to believe,—what the Englishman is always too ready to believe,—that the having a vote, like the having a large family, or a large business, or large muscles, has in itself some edifying and perfecting effect upon human nature. Or else he cries out to the democracy,—"the men," as he calls them, "upon whose shoulders the greatness of England rests,"—he cries out to them: "See what you have done! I look over this country and see the cities you have built, the railroads you have made, the manufactures you have produced, the cargoes which freight the ships of the greatest mercantile navy the world has ever seen! I see that you have converted by your labours what was once a wilderness, these islands, into a fruitful garden; I know that you have created this wealth, and are a nation whose name is a word of power throughout all the world." Why, this is just the very style of laudation with which Mr. Roebuck or Mr. Lowe debauches the minds of the middle classes, and makes such Philistines of them. It is the same fashion of teaching a man to value himself not on what he *is*, not on his progress in sweetness and light, but on the number of the railroads he has constructed, or the bigness of the tabernacle he has built. Only the middle classes are told they have done it all with their energy, self-reliance, and capital, and the democracy are told they have done it all with their hands and sinews. But teaching the democracy to put its trust in achievements of this kind is merely training them to be Philistines to take the place of the Philistines whom they are super-seding; and they too, like the middle class, will be en-couraged to sit down at the banquet of the future with-out having on a wedding garment, and nothing excellent can then come from them. Those who know their be-setting faults, those who have watched them and lis-tened to them, or those who will read the instructive account recently given of them by one of themselves, the *Journeyman Engineer*, will agree that the idea which culture sets before us of perfection,—an increased spirit-ual activity, having for its characters increased sweet-ness, increased light, increased life, increased sympathy, —is an idea which the new democracy needs far more than the idea of the blessedness of the franchise, or the wonderfulness of its own industrial performances.

Other well-meaning friends of this new power are for leading it, not in the old ruts of middle-class Philistinism, but in ways which are naturally alluring to the feet of democracy, though in this country they are novel and untried ways. I may call them the ways of Jacobinism. Violent indignation with the past, abstract systems of renovation applied wholesale, a new doctrine drawn up in black and white for elaborating down to the very smallest details a rational society for the future,—these are the ways of Jacobinism. Mr. Frederic Harrison and other disciples of Comte,—one of them, Mr. Congreve, is an old friend of mine, and I am glad to have an opportunity of publicly expressing my respect for his talents and character,—are among the friends of democracy who are for leading it in paths of this kind. Mr. Frederic Harrison is very hostile to culture, and from a natural enough motive; for culture is the eternal opponent of the two things which are the signal marks of Jacobinism, —its fierceness, and its addiction to an abstract system. Culture is always assigning to system-makers and systems a smaller share in the bent of human destiny than their friends like. A current in people's minds sets towards new ideas; people are dissatisfied with their old narrow stock of Philistine ideas, Anglo-Saxon ideas, or any other; and some man, some Bentham or Comte, who has the real merit of having early and strongly felt and helped the new current, but who brings plenty of narrowness and mistakes of his own into his feeling and help of it, is credited with being the author of the whole current, the fit person to be entrusted with its regulation and to guide the human race.

The excellent German historian of the mythology of

Rome, Preller, relating the introduction at Rome under the Tarquins of the worship of Apollo, the god of light, healing, and reconciliation, will have us observe that it was not so much the Tarquins who brought to Rome the new worship of Apollo, as a current in the mind of the Roman people which set powerfully at that time towards a new worship of this kind, and away from the old run of Latin and Sabine religious ideas. In a similar way, culture directs our attention to the natural current there is in human affairs, and to its continual working, and will not let us rivet our faith upon any one man and his doings. It makes us see not only his good side, but also how much in him was of necessity limited and transient; nay, it even feels a pleasure, a sense of an increased freedom and of an ampler future, in so doing.

I remember, when I was under the influence of a mind to which I feel the greatest obligations, the mind of a man who was the very incarnation of sanity and clear sense, a man the most considerable, it seems to me, whom America has yet produced,—Benjamin Franklin,—I remember the relief with which, after long feeling the sway of Franklin's imperturbable common-sense, I came upon a project of his for a new version of the Book of Job, to replace the old version, the style of which, says Franklin, has become obsolete, and thence less agreeable. "I give," he continues, "a few verses, which may serve as a sample of the kind of version I would recommend." We all recollect the famous verse in our translation: "Then Satan answered the Lord and said: 'Doth Job fear God for nought?'" Franklin makes this: "Does your Majesty imagine that Job's good conduct is the effect of mere personal attachment and affection?" I well remember how, when first I read that, I drew a deep breath of relief, and said to myself: "After all, there is a stretch of humanity beyond Franklin's victorious good sense!" So, after hearing Bentham cried loudly up as the renovator of modern society, and Bentham's mind and ideas proposed as the rulers of our future, I open the *Deontology*. There I read: "While Xenophon was writing his history and Euclid teaching geometry, Socrates and Plato were talking nonsense under pretence of talking wisdom and morality. This morality of theirs consisted in words; this wisdom of theirs was the denial of matters known to every man's experience." From the moment of reading that, I am delivered from the bondage of Bentham! the fanaticism of his adherents can touch me no longer. I feel the inadequacy of his mind and ideas for supplying the rule of human society, for perfection.

Culture tends always thus to deal with the men of a system, of disciples, of a school; with men like Comte, or the late Mr. Buckle, or Mr. Mill. However much it may find to admire in these personages, or in some of them, it nevertheless remembers the text: "Be not ye called Rabbi!" and it soon passes on from any Rabbi. But Jacobinism loves a Rabbi; it does not want to pass on from its Rabbi in pursuit of a future and still unreached perfection; it wants its Rabbi and his ideas to stand for perfection, that they may with the more authority recast the world; and for Jacobinism, therefore, culture,—eternally passing onwards and seeking,—is an impertinence and an offence. But culture, just because it resists this tendency of Jacobinism to impose on us a man with limitations and errors of his own along with the true ideas of which he is the organ, really does the world and Jacobinism itself a service.

So, too, Jacobinism, in its fierce hatred of the past and of those whom it makes liable for the sins of the past, cannot away with the inexhaustible indulgence proper to culture, the consideration of circumstances, the severe judgment of actions joined to the merciful judgment of persons. "The man of culture is in politics," cries Mr. Frederic Harrison, "one of the poorest mortals alive!" Mr. Frederic Harrison wants to be doing business, and he complains that the man of culture stops him with a "turn for small fault-finding, love of selfish ease, and indecision in action." Of what use is culture, he asks, except for "a critic of new books or a professor of *belles lettres?*" Why, it is of use because, in presence of the fierce exasperation which breathes, or rather, I may say, ·hisses through the whole production in which Mr. Frederic Harrison asks that question, it reminds us that the perfection of human nature is sweetness and light. It is of use because, like religion,—that other effort after perfection,—it testifies that, where bitter envying and strife are, there is confusion and every evil work.

The pursuit of perfection, then, is the pursuit of sweetness and light. He who works for sweetness and light, works to make reason and the will of God prevail. He who works for machinery, he who works for hatred, works only for confusion. Culture looks beyond machinery, culture hates hatred; culture has one great passion, the passion for sweetness and light. It has one even yet greater!—the passion for making them *prevail*. It is not satisfied till we *all* come to a perfect man; it knows that the sweetness and light of the few must be imperfect until the raw and unkindled masses of humanity are touched with sweetness and light. If I have not shrunk from saying that we must work for sweetness and light, so neither have I shrunk from saying that we must have a broad basis, must have sweetness and light for as many as possible. Again and again I have insisted how those are the happy moments of humanity, how those are the marking epochs of a people's life, how those are the flowering times for literature and art and all the creative power of genius, when there is a *national* glow of life and thought, when the whole of society is in the fullest measure permeated by thought, sensible to beauty, intelligent and alive. Only it must be *real* thought and *real* beauty; *real* sweetness and *real* light. Plenty of people will try to give the masses, as they call them, an intellectual food prepared and adapted in the way they think proper for the actual condition of the masses. The ordinary popular literature is an example of this way of working on the masses. Plenty of people will try to indoctrinate the masses with the set of ideas and judgments constituting the creed of their own profession or party. Our religious and political organisations give an example of this way of working on the masses. I condemn neither way; but culture works differently. It does not try to teach down to the level of inferior classes; it does not try to win them for this or that sect of its own, with ready-made judgments and watchwords. It seeks to do away with classes; to make the best that has been thought and known in the world current everywhere; to make all men live in an atmosphere of sweetness and light, where they may use ideas, as it uses them itself, freely,—nourished, and not bound by them.

This is the *social idea*; and the men of culture are the true apostles of equality. The great men of culture are those who have had a passion for diffusing, for making prevail, for carrying from one end of society to the other, the best knowledge, the best ideas of their time; who have laboured to divest knowledge of all that was harsh, uncouth, difficult, abstract, professional, exclusive; to humanise it, to make it efficient outside the clique of the cultivated and learned, yet still remaining the *best* knowledge and thought of the time, and a true source, therefore, of sweetness and light. Such a man was Abelard in the Middle Ages, in spite of all his im-

perfections; and thence the boundless emotion and enthusiasm which Abelard excited. Such were Lessing and
Herder in Germany, at the end of the last century; and
their services to Germany were in this way inestimably
precious. Generations will pass, and literary monuments
will accumulate, and works far more perfect than the
works of Lessing and Herder will be produced in Germany; and yet the names of these two men will fill a
German with a reverence and enthusiasm such as the
names of the most gifted masters will hardly awaken.
And why? Because they *humanised* knowledge; because
they broadened the basis of life and intelligence; because they worked powerfully to diffuse sweetness and
light, to make reason and the will of God prevail. With
Saint Augustine they said: "Let us not leave thee alone
to make in the secret of thy knowledge, as thou didst
before the creation of the firmament, the division of
light from darkness; let the children of thy spirit, placed
in their firmament, make their light shine upon the
earth, mark the division of night and day, and announce
the revolution of the times; for the old order is passed,
and the new arises; the night is spent, the day is come
forth; and thou shalt crown the year with thy blessing,
when thou shalt send forth labourers into thy harvest
sown by other hands than theirs; when thou shalt send
forth new labourers to new seed-times, whereof the harvest shall be not yet."

II. DOING AS ONE LIKES

I have been trying to show that culture is, or ought to
be, the study and pursuit of perfection; and that of
perfection as pursued by culture, beauty and intelligence, or, in other words, sweetness and light, are the

main characters. But hitherto I have been insisting chiefly on beauty, or sweetness, as a character of perfection. To complete rightly my design, it evidently remains to speak also of intelligence, or light, as a character of perfection.

First, however, I ought perhaps to notice that, both here and on the other side of the Atlantic, all sorts of objections are raised against the "religion of culture," as the objectors mockingly call it, which I am supposed to be promulgating. It is said to be a religion proposing parmaceti, or some scented salve or other, as a cure for human miseries; a religion breathing a spirit of cultivated inaction, making its believer refuse to lend a hand at uprooting the definite evils on all sides of us, and filling him with antipathy against the reforms and reformers which try to extirpate them. In general, it is summed up as being not practical, or,—as some critics familiarly put it,—all moonshine. That Alcibiades, the editor of the *Morning Star*, taunts me, as its promulgator, with living out of the world and knowing nothing of life and men. That great austere toiler, the editor of the *Daily Telegraph*, upbraids me,—but kindly, and more in sorrow than in anger,—for trifling with æsthetics and poetical fancies, while he himself, in that arsenal of his in Fleet Street, is bearing the burden and heat of the day. An intelligent American newspaper, the *Nation*, says that it is very easy to sit in one's study and find fault with the course of modern society, but the thing is to propose practical improvements for it. While, finally, Mr. Frederic Harrison, in a very good-tempered and witty satire, which makes me quite understand his having apparently achieved such a conquest of my young Prussian friend, Arminius, at last gets moved to an almost stern moral impatience, to behold, as he says,

"Death, sin, cruelty stalk among us, filling their maws with innocence and youth," and me, in the midst of the general tribulation, handing out my pouncet-box.

It is impossible that all these remonstrances and re-proofs should not affect me, and I shall try my very best, in completing my design and in speaking of light as one of the characters of perfection, and of culture as giving us light, to profit by the objections I have heard and read, and to drive at practice as much as I can, by show-ing the communications and passages into practical life from the doctrine which I am inculcating.

It is said that a man with my theories of sweetness and light is full of antipathy against the rougher or coarser movements going on around him, that he will not lend a hand to the humble operation of uprooting evil by their means, and that therefore the believers in action grow impatient with him. But what if rough and coarse action, ill-calculated action, action with insuffi-cient light, is, and has for a long time been, our bane? What if our urgent want now is, not to act at any price, but rather to lay in a stock of light for our difficulties? In that case, to refuse to lend a hand to the rougher and coarser movements going on round us, to make the primary need, both for oneself and others, to consist in enlightening ourselves and qualifying ourselves to act less at random, is surely the best and in real truth the most practical line our endeavours can take. So that if I can show what my opponents call rough or coarse ac-tion, but what I would rather call random and ill-regu-lated action,—action with insufficient light, action pur-sued because we like to be doing something and doing it as we please, and do not like the trouble of thinking and the severe constraint of any kind of rule,—if I can show this to be, at the present moment, a practical mis-chief and dangerous to us, then I have found a practical use for light in correcting this state of things, and have only to exemplify how, in cases which fall under everybody's observation, it may deal with it.

When I began to speak of culture, I insisted on our bondage to machinery, on our proneness to value machinery as an end in itself, without looking beyond it to the end for which alone, in truth, it is valuable. Freedom, I said, was one of those things which we thus worshipped in itself, without enough regarding the ends for which freedom is to be desired. In our common notions and talk about freedom, we eminently show our idolatry of machinery. Our prevalent notion is,—and I quoted a number of instances to prove it,—that it is a most happy and important thing for a man merely to be able to do as he likes. On what he is to do when he is thus free to do as he likes, we do not lay so much stress. Our familiar praise of the British Constitution under which we live, is that it is a system of checks,—a system which stops and paralyses any power in interfering with the free action of individuals. To this effect Mr. Bright, who loves to walk in the old ways of the Constitution, said forcibly in one of his great speeches, what many other people are every day saying less forcibly, that the central idea of English life and politics is *the assertion of personal liberty*. Evidently this is so; but evidently, also, as feudalism, which with its ideas and habits of subordination was for many centuries silently behind the British Constitution, dies out, and we are left with nothing but our system of checks, and our notion of its being the great right and happiness of an Englishman to do as far as possible what he likes, we are in danger of drifting towards anarchy. We have not the notion, so familiar on the Continent and to antiquity, of *the State*,—the nation in its collective and corporate character, entrusted with stringent powers for the general advantage, and

controlling individual wills in the name of an interest
wider than that of individuals. We say, what is very
true, that this notion is often made instrumental to
tyranny; we say that a State is in reality made up of the
individuals who compose it, and that every individual is
the best judge of his own interests. Our leading class is
an aristocracy, and no aristocracy likes the notion of a
State-authority greater than itself, with a stringent administrative machinery superseding the decorative inutilities of lord-lieutenancy, deputy-lieutenancy, and the
posse comitatus, which are all in its own hands. Our
middle class, the great representative of trade and Dissent, with its maxims of every man for himself in business, every man for himself in religion, dreads a powerful administration which might somehow interfere with
it; and besides, it has its own decorative inutilities of
vestrymanship and guardianship, which are to this class
what lord-lieutenancy and the county magistracy are
to the aristocratic class, and a stringent administration
might either take these functions out of its hands, or
prevent its exercising them in its own comfortable, independent manner, as at present.

Then as to our working class. This class, pressed constantly by the hard daily compulsion of material wants,
is naturally the very centre and stronghold of our national idea, that it is man's ideal right and felicity to do
as he likes. I think I have somewhere related how M.
Michelet said to me of the people of France, that it was
"a nation of barbarians civilised by the conscription." He
meant that through their military service the idea of
public duty and of discipline was brought to the mind of
these masses, in other respects so raw and uncultivated.
Our masses are quite as raw and uncultivated as the
French; and so far from their having the idea of public
duty and of discipline, superior to the individual's self-

will, brought to their mind by a universal obligation of military service, such as that of the conscription,—so far from their having this, the very idea of a conscription is so at variance with our English notion of the prime right and blessedness of doing as one likes, that I remember the manager of the Clay Cross works in Derbyshire told me during the Crimean war, when our want of soldiers was much felt and some people were talking of a conscription, that sooner than submit to a conscription the population of that district would flee to the mines, and lead a sort of Robin Hood life under ground.

For a long time, as I have said, the strong feudal habits of subordination and deference continued to tell upon the working class. The modern spirit has now almost entirely dissolved those habits, and the anarchical tendency of our worship of freedom in and for itself, of our superstitious faith, as I say, in machinery, is becoming very manifest. More and more, because of this our blind faith in machinery, because of our want of light to enable us to look beyond machinery to the end for which machinery is valuable, this and that man, and this and that body of men, all over the country, are beginning to assert and put in practice an Englishman's right to do what he likes; his right to march where he likes, meet where he likes, enter where he likes, hoot as he likes, threaten as he likes, smash as he likes. All this, I say, tends to anarchy; and though a number of excellent people, and particularly my friends of the Liberal or progressive party, as they call themselves, are kind enough to reassure us by saying that these are trifles, that a few transient outbreaks of rowdyism signify nothing, that our system of liberty is one which itself cures all the evils which it works, that the educated and intelligent classes stand in overwhelming

strength and majestic repose, ready, like our military
force in riots, to act at a moment's notice,—yet one finds
that one's Liberal friends generally say this because they
have such faith in themselves and their nostrums, when
they shall return, as the public welfare requires, to place
and power. But this faith of theirs one cannot exactly
share, when one has so long had them and their nostrums at work, and sees that they have not prevented
our coming to our present embarrassed condition. And
one finds, also, that the outbreaks of rowdyism tend to
become less and less of trifles, to become more frequent
rather than less frequent; and that meanwhile our educated and intelligent classes remain in their majestic'
repose, and somehow or other, whatever happens, their
overwhelming strength, like our military force in riots,
never does act.

How, indeed, *should* their overwhelming strength
act, when the man who gives an inflammatory lecture,
or breaks down the park railings, or invades a Secretary of State's office, is only following an Englishman's
impulse to do as he likes; and our own conscience
tells us that we ourselves have always regarded this
impulse as something primary and sacred? Mr. Murphy
lectures at Birmingham, and showers on the Catholic
population of that town "words," says the Home Secretary, "only fit to be addressed to thieves or murderers."
What then? Mr. Murphy has his own reasons of several
kinds. He suspects the Roman Catholic Church of de-
signs upon Mrs. Murphy; and he says if mayors and
magistrates do not care for their wives and daughters,
he does. But, above all, he is doing as he likes; or, in
worthier language, asserting his personal liberty. "I will
carry out my lectures if they walk over my body as a
dead corpse; and I say to the Mayor of Birmingham
that he is my servant while I am in Birmingham, and as

my servant he must do his duty and protect me." Touching and beautiful words, which find a sympathetic chord in every British bosom! The moment it is plainly put before us that a man is asserting his personal liberty, we are half disarmed; because we are believers in freedom, and not in some dream of a right reason to which the assertion of our freedom is to be subordinated. Accordingly, the Secretary of State had to say that although the lecturer's language was "only fit to be addressed to thieves or murderers," yet, "I do not think he is to be deprived, I do not think that anything I have said could justify the inference that he is to be deprived, of the right of protection in a place built by him for the purpose of these lectures; because the language was not language which afforded grounds for a criminal prosecution." No, nor to be silenced by Mayor, or Home Secretary, or any administrative authority on earth, simply on their notion of what is discreet and reasonable! This is in perfect consonance with our public opinion, and with our national love for the assertion of personal liberty.

In quite another department of affairs, an experienced and distinguished Chancery Judge relates an incident which is just to the same effect as this of Mr. Murphy. A testator bequeathed £300 a year, to be for ever applied as a pension to some person who had been unsuccessful in literature, and whose duty should be to support and diffuse, by his writings, the testator's own views, as enforced in the testator's publications. The views were not worth a straw, and the bequest was appealed against in the Court of Chancery on the ground of its absurdity; but, being only absurd, it was upheld, and the so-called charity was established. Having, I say, at the bottom of our English hearts a very strong belief in freedom, and a very weak belief in right reason, we are soon silenced

when a man pleads the prime right to do as he likes, because this is the prime right for ourselves too; and even
if we attempt now and then to mumble something about
reason, yet we have ourselves thought so little about
this and so much about liberty, that we are in conscience forced, when our brother Philistine with whom
we are meddling turns boldly round upon us and asks:
Have you any light?—to shake our heads ruefully, and
to let him go his own way after all.

There are many things to be said on behalf of this
exclusive attention of ours to liberty, and of the relaxed
habits of government which it has engendered. It is very
easy to mistake or to exaggerate the sort of anarchy from
which we are in danger through them. We are not in
danger from Fenianism, fierce and turbulent as it may
show itself; for against this our conscience is free enough
to let us act resolutely and put forth our overwhelming
strength the moment there is any real need for it. In
the first place, it never was any part of our creed that
the great right and blessedness of an Irishman, or, indeed, of anybody on earth except an Englishman, is to
do as he likes; and we can have no scruple at all about
abridging, if necessary, a non-Englishman's assertion of
personal liberty. The British Constitution, its checks, and
its prime virtues, are for Englishmen. We may extend
them to others out of love and kindness; but we find no
real divine law written on our hearts constraining us so
to extend them. And then the difference between an
Irish Fenian and an English rough is so immense, and
the case, in dealing with the Fenian, so much more
clear! He is so evidently desperate and dangerous, a
man of a conquered race, a Papist, with centuries of
ill-usage to inflame him against us, with an alien religion
established in his country by us at his expense, with no
admiration of our institutions, no love of our virtues, no

talents for our business, no turn for our comfort! Show him our symbolical Truss Manufactory on the finest site in Europe, and tell him that British industrialism and individualism can bring a man to that, and he remains cold! Evidently, if we deal tenderly with a sentimentalist like this, it is out of pure philanthropy.

But with the Hyde Park rioter how different! He is our own flesh and blood; he is a Protestant; he is framed by nature to do as we do, hate what we hate, love what we love; he is capable of feeling the symbolical force of the Truss Manufactory; the question of questions, for him, is a wages question. That beautiful sentence Sir Daniel Gooch quoted to the Swindon workmen, and which I treasure as Mrs. Gooch's Golden Rule, or the Divine Injunction "Be ye Perfect" done into British,—the sentence Sir Daniel Gooch's mother repeated to him every morning when he was a boy going to work:—*"Ever remember, my dear Dan, that you should look forward to being some day manager of that concern!"*—this truthful maxim is perfectly fitted to shine forth in the heart of the Hyde Park rough also, and to be his guiding-star through life. He has no visionary schemes of revolution and transformation, though of course he would like his class to rule, as the aristocratic class like their class to rule, and the middle class theirs. But meanwhile our social machine is a little out of order; there are a good many people in our paradisiacal centres of industrialism and individualism taking the bread out of one another's mouths. The rough has not yet quite found his groove and settled down to his work, and so he is just asserting his personal liberty a little, going where he likes, assembling where he likes, bawling as he likes, hustling as he likes. Just as the rest of us,—as the country squires in the aristocratic class, as the political dissenters in the middle class,—he has no idea of a

State, of the nation in its collective and corporate character controlling, as government, the free swing of this or that one of its members in the name of the higher reason of all of them, his own as well as that of others. He sees the rich, the aristocratic class, in occupation of the executive government, and so if he is stopped from making Hyde Park a bear-garden or the streets impassable, he says he is being butchered by the aristocracy.

His apparition is somewhat embarrassing, because too many cooks spoil the broth; because, while the aristocratic and middle classes have long been doing as they like with great vigour, he has been too undeveloped and submissive hitherto to join in the game; and now, when he does come, he comes in immense numbers, and is rather raw and rough. But he does not break many laws, or not many at one time; and, as our laws were made for very different circumstances from our present (but always with an eye to Englishmen doing as they like), and as the clear letter of the law must be against our Englishman who does as he likes and not only the spirit of the law and public policy, and as Government must neither have any discretionary power nor act resolutely on its own interpretation of the law if any one disputes it, it is evident our laws give our playful giant, in doing as he likes, considerable advantage. Besides, even if he can be clearly proved to commit an illegality in doing as he likes, there is always the resource of not putting the law in force, or of abolishing it. So he has his way, and if he has his way he is soon satisfied for the time. However, he falls into the habit of taking it oftener and oftener, and at last begins to create by his operations a confusion of which mischievous people can take advantage, and which, at any rate, by troubling the common course of business throughout the country, tends to cause distress, and so to increase the sort of anarchy and social disintegration which had previously commenced. And thus that profound sense of settled order and security, without which a society like ours cannot live and grow at all, sometimes seems to be beginning to threaten us with taking its departure.

Now, if culture, which simply means trying to perfect oneself, and one's mind as part of oneself, brings us light, and if light shows us that there is nothing so very blessed in merely doing as one likes, that the worship of the mere freedom to do as one likes is worship of machinery, that the really blessed thing is to like what right reason ordains, and to follow her authority, then we have got a practical benefit out of culture. We have got a much wanted principle, a principle of authority, to counteract the tendency to anarchy which seems to be threatening us.

But how to organise this authority, or to what hands to entrust the wielding of it? How to get your *State*, summing up the right reason of the community, and giving effect to it, as circumstances may require, with vigour? And here I think I see my enemies waiting for me with a hungry joy in their eyes. But I shall elude them.

The *State*, the power most representing the right reason of the nation, and most worthy, therefore, of ruling, —of exercising, when circumstances require it, authority over us all,—is for Mr. Carlyle the aristocracy. For Mr. Lowe, it is the middle class with its incomparable Parliament. For the Reform League, it is the working class, the class with "the brightest powers of sympathy and readiest powers of action." Now culture, with its disinterested pursuit of perfection, culture, simply trying to see things as they are in order to seize on the best and to make it prevail, is surely well fitted to help us to judge rightly, by all the aids of observing, reading, and thinking, the qualifications and titles to our confidence of these three candidates for authority, and can thus render us a practical service of no mean value.

So when Mr. Carlyle, a man of genius to whom we have all at one time or other been indebted for refreshment and stimulus, says we should give rule to the aristocracy, mainly because of its dignity and politeness, surely culture is useful in reminding us, that in our idea of perfection the characters of beauty and intelligence are both of them present, and sweetness and light, the two noblest of things, are united. Allowing, therefore, with Mr. Carlyle, the aristocratic class to possess sweetness, culture insists on the necessity of light also, and shows us that aristocracies, being by the very nature of things inaccessible to ideas, unapt to see how the world is going, must be somewhat wanting in light, and must therefore be, at a moment when light is our great requisite, inadequate to our needs. Aristocracies, those children of the established fact, are for epochs of concentration. In epochs of expansion, epochs such as that in which we now live, epochs when always the warning voice is again heard: *Now is the judgment of this world,* —in such epochs aristocracies with their natural clinging to the established fact, their want of sense for the flux of things, for the inevitable transitoriness of all human institutions, are bewildered and helpless. Their serenity, their high spirit, their power of haughty resistance,—the great qualities of an aristocracy, and the secret of its distinguished manners and dignity,—these very qualities, in an epoch of expansion, turn against their possessors. Again and again I have said how the refinement of an aristocracy may be precious and educative to a raw nation as a kind of shadow of true refinement; how its serenity and dignified freedom from petty cares may serve as a useful foil to set off the vulgarity and hideousness of that type of life which a hard middle class tends to establish, and to help people to see this vulgarity and hideousness in their true colours. But the true grace and serenity is that of which Greece and Greek art suggest the admirable ideals of perfection,— a serenity which comes from having made order among ideas and harmonised them; whereas the serenity of aristocracies, at least the peculiar serenity of aristocracies of Teutonic origin, appears to come from their never having had any ideas to trouble them. And so, in a time of expansion like the present, a time for ideas, one gets perhaps, in regarding an aristocracy, even more than the idea of serenity, the idea of futility and sterility.

One has often wondered whether upon the whole earth there is anything so unintelligent, so unapt to perceive how the world is really going, as an ordinary young Englishman of our upper class. Ideas he has not, and neither has he that seriousness of our middle class which is, as I have often said, the great strength of this class, and may become its salvation. Why, a man may hear a young Dives of the aristocratic class, when the whim takes him to sing the praises of wealth and material comfort, sing them with a cynicism from which the conscience of the veriest Philistine of our industrial middle class would recoil in affright. And when, with the natural sympathy of aristocracies for firm dealing with the multitude, and his uneasiness at our feeble dealing with it at home, an unvarnished young Englishman of our aristocratic class applauds the absolute rulers on the Continent, he in general manages completely to miss the grounds of reason and intelligence which alone can give any colour of justification, any possibility of existence, to those rulers, and applauds them on grounds which it would make their own hair stand on end to listen to.

And all this time we are in an epoch of expansion; and the essence of an epoch of expansion is a movement of ideas, and the one salvation of an epoch of expansion is a harmony of ideas. The very principle of the authority which we are seeking as a defence against anarchy is right reason, ideas, light. The more, therefore, an aristocracy calls to its aid its innate forces,—its impenetrability, its high spirit, its power of haughty resistance, —to deal with an epoch of expansion, the graver is the danger, the greater the certainty of explosion, the surer the aristocracy's defeat; for it is trying to do violence to nature instead of working along with it. The best powers shown by the best men of an aristocracy at such an epoch are, it will be observed, non-aristocratical powers, powers of industry, powers of intelligence; and these powers thus exhibited, tend really not to strengthen the aristocracy, but to take their owners out of it, to expose them to the dissolving agencies of thought and change, to make them men of the modern spirit and of the future. If, as sometimes happens, they add to their non-aristocratical qualities of labour and thought, a strong dose of aristocratical qualities also,—of pride, defiance, turn for resistance,—this truly aristocratical side of them, so far from adding any strength to them, really neutralises their force and makes them impracticable and ineffective.

Knowing myself to be indeed sadly to seek, as one of my many critics says, in "a philosophy with coherent, interdependent, subordinate, and derivative principles," I continually have recourse to a plain man's expedient of trying to make what few simple notions I have, clearer and more intelligible to myself by means of example and illustration. And having been brought up at Oxford in the bad old times, when we were stuffed with Greek and Aristotle, and thought nothing of preparing ourselves by the study of modern languages,—as after Mr. Lowe's great speech at Edinburgh we shall do,—to fight the battle of life with the waiters in foreign hotels, my head is still full of a lumber of phrases we learnt at Oxford from Aristotle, about virtue being in a mean, and about excess and defect, and so on. Once when I had had the advantage of listening to the Reform debates in the House of Commons, having heard a number of interesting speakers, and among them a well-known lord and a well-known baronet, I remember it struck me, applying Aristotle's machinery of the mean to my ideas about our aristocracy, that the lord was exactly the perfection, or happy mean, or virtue, of aristocracy, and the baronet the excess. And I fancied that by observing these two we might see both the inadequacy of aristocracy to supply the principle of authority needful for our present wants, and the danger of its trying to supply it when it was not really competent for the business. On the one hand, in the brilliant lord, showing plenty of high spirit, but remarkable, far above and beyond his gift of high spirit, for the fine tempering of his high spirit, for ease, serenity, politeness,—the great virtues, as Mr. Carlyle says, of aristocracy,—in this beautiful and virtuous mean, there seemed evidently some insufficiency of light; while, on the other hand, the worthy baronet, in whom the high spirit of aristocracy, its impenetrability, defiant courage, and pride of resistance, were developed even in excess, was manifestly capable, if he had his way given him, of causing us great danger, and, indeed, of throwing the whole commonwealth into confusion. Then I reverted to that old fundamental notion of mine about the grand merit of our race being really our honesty. And the very helplessness of our aristocratic or governing class in dealing with our perturbed social condition, their jealousy of entrusting too

much power to the State as it now actually exists—that
is to themselves—gave me a sort of pride and satisfaction; because I saw they were, as a whole, too honest
to try and manage a business for which they did not
feel themselves capable.

Surely, now, it is no inconsiderable boon which culture confers upon us, if in embarrassed times like the
present it enables us to look at the ins and the outs of
things in this way, without hatred and without partial-
ity, and with a disposition to see the good in everybody
all round. And I try to follow just the same course with
our middle class as with our aristocracy. Mr. Lowe talks
to us of this strong middle part of the nation, of the unrivalled deeds of our Liberal middle-class Parliament, of
the noble, the heroic work it has performed in the last
thirty years; and I begin to ask myself if we shall not,
then, find in our middle class the principle of authority
we want, and if we had not better take administration
as well as legislation away from the weak extreme which
now administers for us, and commit both to the strong
middle part. I observe, too, that the heroes of middle-
class liberalism, such as we have hitherto known it,
speak with a kind of prophetic anticipation of the great
destiny which awaits them, and as if the future was
clearly theirs. The advanced party, the progressive party,
the party in alliance with the future, are the names they
like to give themselves. "The principles which will obtain
recognition in the future," says Mr. Miall, a personage
of deserved eminence among the political Dissenters, as
they are called, who have been the backbone of middle-
class liberalism,—"the principles which will obtain recognition in the future are the principles for which I have
long and zealously laboured. I qualified myself for join-
ing in the work of harvest by doing to the best of my
ability the duties of seedtime." These duties, if one is

to gather them from the works of the great Liberal party in the last thirty years, are, as I have elsewhere summed them up, the advocacy of free trade, of Parliamentary reform, of abolition of church-rates, of voluntaryism in religion and education, of non-interference of the State between employers and employed, and of marriage with one's deceased wife's sister.

Now I know, when I object that all this is machinery, the great Liberal middle class has by this time grown cunning enough to answer that it always meant more by these things than meets the eye; that it has had that within which passes show, and that we are soon going to see, in a Free Church and all manner of good things, what it was. But I have learned from Bishop Wilson (if Mr. Frederic Harrison will forgive my again quoting that poor old hierophant of a decayed superstition): "If we would really know our heart let us impartially view our actions"; and I cannot help thinking that if our Liberals had had so much sweetness and light in their inner minds as they allege, more of it must have come out in their sayings and doings.

An American friend of the English Liberals says, indeed, that their Dissidence of Dissent has been a mere instrument of the political Dissenters for making reason and the will of God prevail (and no doubt he would say the same of marriage with one's deceased wife's sister); and that the abolition of a State Church is merely the Dissenter's means to this end, just as culture is mine. Another American defender of theirs says just the same of their industrialism and free trade; indeed, this gentleman, taking the bull by the horns, proposes that we should for the future call industrialism culture, and the industrialists the men of culture, and then of course there can be no longer any misapprehension about their true character; and besides the pleasure of being wealthy and comfortable, they will have authentic recognition as vessels of sweetness and light.

All this is undoubtedly specious; but I must remark that the culture of which I talked was an endeavour to come at reason and the will of God by means of reading, observing, and thinking; and that whoever calls anything else culture, may, indeed, call it so if he likes, but then he talks of something quite different from what I talked of. And, again, as culture's way of working for reason and the will of God is by directly trying to know more about them, while the Dissidence of Dissent is evidently in itself no effort of this kind, nor is its Free Church, in fact, a church with worthier conceptions of God and the ordering of the world than the State Church professes, but with mainly the same conceptions of these as the State Church has, only that every man is to comport himself as he likes in professing them,—this being so, I cannot at once accept the Nonconformity any more than the industrialism and the other great works of our Liberal middle class as proof positive that this class is in possession of light, and that here is the true seat of authority for which we are in search; but I must try a little further, and seek for other indications which may enable me to make up my mind.

Why should we not do with the middle class as we have done with the aristocratic class,—find in it some representative men who may stand for the virtuous mean of this class, for the perfection of its present qualities and mode of being, and also for the excess of them. Such men must clearly not be men of genius like Mr. Bright; for, as I have formerly said, so far as a man has genius he tends to take himself out of the category of class altogether, and to become simply a man. Some more ordinary man would be more to the purpose,— would sum up better in himself, without disturbing influences, the general liberal force of the middle class, the force by which it has done its great works of free trade, Parliamentary reform, voluntaryism, and so on, and the spirit in which it has done them. Now it happens that a typical middle-class man, the member for one of our chief industrial cities, has given us a famous sentence which bears directly on the resolution of our present question: whether there is light enough in our middle class to make it the proper seat of the authority we wish to establish. When there was a talk some little while ago about the state of middle-class education, our friend, as the representative of that class, spoke some memorable words:—"There had been a cry that middle-class education ought to receive more attention. He confessed himself very much surprised by the clamour that was raised. He did not think that class need excite the sympathy either of the legislature or the public." Now this satisfaction of our middle-class member of Parliament with the mental state of the middle class was truly representative, and makes good his claim to stand as the beautiful and virtuous mean of that class. But it is obviously at variance with our definition of culture, or the pursuit of light and perfection, which made light and perfection consist, not in resting and being, but in growing and becoming, in a perpetual advance in beauty and wisdom. So the middle class is by its essence, as one may say, by its incomparable self-satisfaction decisively expressed through its beautiful and virtuous mean, self-excluded from wielding an authority of which light is to be the very soul.

Clear as this is, it will be made clearer still if we take some representative man as the excess of the middle class, and remember that the middle class, in general, is to be conceived as a body swaying between the qualities of its mean and of its excess, and on the whole, of course, as human nature is constituted, inclining rather towards the excess than the mean. Of its excess no better representative can possibly be imagined than a Dissenting minister from Walsall, who came before the public in connection with the proceedings at Birmingham of Mr. Murphy, already mentioned. Speaking in the midst of an irritated population of Catholics, this Walsall gentleman exclaimed: "I say, then, away with the Mass! It is from the bottomless pit; and in the bottomless pit shall all liars have their part, in the lake that burneth with fire and brimstone." And again: "When all the praties were black in Ireland, why didn't the priests say the hocus-pocus over them, and make them all good again?" He shared, too, Mr. Murphy's fears of some invasion of his domestic happiness: "What I wish to say to you as Protestant husbands is, *Take care of your wives!*" And finally, in the true vein of an Englishman doing as he likes, a vein of which I have at some length pointed out the present dangers, he recommended for imitation the example of some churchwardens at Dublin, among whom, said he, "there was a Luther and also a Melanchthon," who had made very short work with some ritualist or other, hauled him down from his pulpit, and kicked him out of church. Now it is manifest, as I said in the case of our aristocratical baronet, that if we let this excess of the sturdy English middle class, this conscientious Protestant Dissenter, so strong, so self-reliant, so fully persuaded in his own mind, have his way, he would be capable, with his want of light,—or, to use the language of the religious world, with his zeal without knowledge, —of stirring up strife which neither he nor any one else could easily compose.

And then comes in, as it did also with the aristocracy, the honesty of our race, and by the voice of another middle-class man, Alderman of the City of London and

Colonel of the City of London Militia, proclaims that it
has twinges of conscience, and that it will not attempt
to cope with our social disorders, and to deal with a
business which it feels to be too high for it. Every one remembers how this virtuous Alderman-Colonel, or Colo-
nel-Alderman, led his militia through the London streets;
how the bystanders gathered to see him pass; how the
London roughs, asserting an Englishman's best and
most blissful right of doing what he likes, robbed and
beat the bystanders; and how the blameless warrior-mag-
istrate refused to let his troops interfere. "The crowd,"
he touchingly said afterwards, "was mostly composed
of fine healthy strong men, bent on mischief; if he had
allowed his soldiers to interfere they might have been
overpowered, their rifles taken from them and used
against them by the mob; a riot, in fact, might have en-
sued, and been attended with bloodshed, compared with
which the assaults and loss of property that actually oc-
curred would have been as nothing." Honest and affecting testimony of the English middle class to its own
inadequacy for the authoritative part one's admiration
would sometimes incline one to assign to it! "Who are
we," they say by the voice of their Alderman-Colonel,
"that we should not be overpowered if we attempt to
cope with social anarchy, our rifles taken from us and
used against us by the mob, and we, perhaps, robbed
and beaten ourselves? Or what light have we, beyond a
free-born Englishman's impulse to do as he likes, which
could justify us in preventing, at the cost of bloodshed,
other free-born Englishmen from doing as they like, and
robbing and beating us as much as they please?"

This distrust of themselves as an adequate centre of
authority does not mark the working class, as was shown
by their readiness the other day in Hyde Park to take
upon themselves all the functions of government. But

this comes from the working class being, as I have often said, still an embryo, of which no one can yet quite foresee the final development; and from its not having the same experience and self-knowledge as the aristocratic and middle classes. Honesty it no doubt has, just like the other classes of Englishmen, but honesty in an inchoate and untrained state; and meanwhile its powers of action, which are, as Mr. Frederic Harrison says, exceedingly ready, easily run away with it. That it cannot at present have a sufficiency of light which comes by culture,—that is, by reading, observing, and thinking,—is clear from the very nature of its condition; and, indeed, we saw that Mr. Frederic Harrison, in seeking to make a free stage for its bright powers of sympathy and ready powers of action, had to begin by throwing overboard culture, and flouting it as only fit for a professor of *belles-lettres*. Still, to make it perfectly manifest that no more in the working class than in the aristocratic and middle classes can one find an adequate centre of authority,—that is, as culture teaches us to conceive our required authority, of light,—let us again follow, with this class, the method we have followed with the aristocratic and middle classes, and try to bring before our minds representative men, who may figure to us its virtue and its excess.

We must not take, of course, men like the chiefs of the Hyde Park demonstration, Colonel Dickson or Mr. Beales; because Colonel Dickson, by his martial profession and dashing exterior, seems to belong properly, like Julius Cæsar and Mirabeau and other great popular leaders, to the aristocratic class, and to be carried into the popular ranks only by his ambition or his genius; while Mr. Beales belongs to our solid middle class, and, perhaps, if he had not been a great popular leader, would have been a Philistine. But Mr. Odger, whose speeches we have all read, and of whom his friends relate, besides, much that is favourable, may very well stand for the beautiful and virtuous mean of our present working class; and I think everybody will admit that in Mr. Odger there is manifestly, with all his good points, some insufficiency of light. The excess of the working class, in its present state of development, is perhaps best shown in Mr. Bradlaugh, the iconoclast, who seems to be almost for baptizing us all in blood and fire into his new social dispensation, and to whose reflections, now that I have once been set going on Bishop Wilson's track, I cannot forbear commending this maxim of the good old man: "Intemperance in talk makes a dreadful havoc in the heart." Mr. Bradlaugh, like our types of excess in the aristocratic and middle classes, is evidently capable, if he had his head given him, of running us all into great dangers and confusion. I conclude, therefore,—what indeed, few of those who do me the honour to read this disquisition are likely to dispute,—that we can as little find in the working class as in the aristocratic or in the middle class our much-wanted source of authority, as culture suggests it to us.

Well, then, what if we tried to rise above the idea of class to the idea of the whole community, *the State*, and to find our centre of light and authority there? Every one of us has the idea of country, as a sentiment; hardly any one of us has the idea of *the State*, as a working power. And why? Because we habitually live in our ordinary selves, which do not carry us beyond the ideas and wishes of the class to which we happen to belong. And we are all afraid of giving to the State too much power, because we only conceive of the State as something equivalent to the class in occupation of the executive government, and are afraid of that class abusing power to its own purposes. If we strengthen the State with the aristocratic class in occupation of the executive government, we imagine we are delivering ourselves up captive to the ideas and wishes of our fierce aristocratical baronet; if with the middle class in occupation of the executive government, to those of our truculent middle-class Dissenting minister; if with the working class, to those of its notorious tribune, Mr. Bradlaugh. And with much justice; owing to the exaggerated notion which we English, as I have said, entertain of the right and blessedness of the mere doing as one likes, of the affirming oneself, and oneself just as it is. People of the aristocratic class want to affirm their ordinary selves, their likings and dislikings; people of the middle class the same, people of the working class the same. By our every day selves, however, we are separate, personal, at war; we are only safe from one another's tyranny when no one has any power; and this safety, in its turn, cannot save us from anarchy. And when, therefore, anarchy presents itself as a danger to us, we know not where to turn.

But by our *best self* we are united, impersonal, at harmony. We are in no peril from giving authority to this, because it is the truest friend we all of us can have; and when anarchy is a danger to us, to this authority we may turn with sure trust. Well, and this is the very self which culture, or the study of perfection, seeks to develop in us; at the expense of our old untransformed self, taking pleasure only in doing what it likes or is used to do, and exposing us to the risk of clashing with every one else who is doing the same! So that our poor culture, which is flouted as so unpractical, leads us to the very ideas capable of meeting the great want of our present embarrassed times! We want an authority, and we find nothing but jealous classes, checks, and a deadlock; culture suggests the idea of *the State*. We find no basis for a firm State-power in our ordinary selves; culture suggests one to us in our *best self*.

It cannot but acutely try a tender conscience to be accused, in a practical country like ours, of keeping aloof from the work and hope of a multitude of earnest-hearted men, and of merely toying with poetry and æsthetics. So it is with no little sense of relief that I find myself thus in the position of one who makes a contribution in aid of the practical necessities of our times. The great thing, it will be observed, is to find our *best* self, and to seek to affirm nothing but that; not,—as we English with our over-value for merely being free and busy have been so accustomed to do,—resting satisfied with a self which comes uppermost long before our best self, and affirming that with blind energy. In short,—to go back yet once more to Bishop Wilson,—of these two excellent rules of Bishop Wilson's for a man's guidance: "Firstly, never go against the best light you have; secondly, take care that your light be not darkness," we English have followed with praiseworthy zeal the first rule, but we have not given so much heed to the second. We have gone manfully according to the best light we have; but we have not taken enough care that this should be really the best light possible for us, that it should not be darkness. And, our honesty being very great, conscience has whispered to us that the light we were following, our ordinary self, was, indeed, perhaps, only an inferior self, only darkness; and that it would not do to impose this seriously on all the world.

But our best self inspires faith, and is capable of affording a serious principle of authority. For example. We are on our way to what the late Duke of Wellington, with his strong sagacity, foresaw and admirably described as "a revolution by due course of law." This is undoubtedly,—if we are still to live and grow, and this famous nation is not to stagnate and dwindle away on the one hand, or, on the other, to perish miserably in mere anarchy and confusion,—what we are on the way to. Great changes there must be, for a revolution cannot accomplish itself without great changes; yet order there must be, for without order a revolution cannot accomplish itself by due course of law. So whatever brings risk of tumult and disorder, multitudinous processions in the streets of our crowded towns, multitudinous meetings in their public places and parks,—demonstrations perfectly unnecessary in the present course of our affairs,—our best self, or right reason, plainly enjoins us to set our faces against. It enjoins us to encourage and uphold the occupants of the executive power, whoever they may be, in firmly prohibiting them. But it does this clearly and resolutely, and is thus a real principle of authority, because it does it with a free conscience; because in thus provisionally strengthening the executive power, it knows that it is not doing this merely to enable our aristocratical baronet to affirm himself as against our working-men's tribune, or our middle-class Dissenter to affirm himself as against both. It knows that it is establishing *the State*, or organ of our collective best self, of our national right reason. And it has the testimony of conscience that it is stablishing the State on behalf of whatever great changes are needed, just as much as on behalf of order; stablishing it to deal just as stringently, when the time comes, with our baronet's aristocratical prejudices, or with the fanaticism of our middle-class Dissenter, as it deals with Mr. Bradlaugh's street-processions.

III. BARBARIANS, PHILISTINES, POPULACE

From a man without a philosophy no one can expect philosophical completeness. Therefore I may observe without shame, that in trying to get a distinct notion of our aristocratic, our middle, and our working class, with a view of testing the claims of each of these classes to become a centre of authority, I have omitted, I find, to complete the old-fashioned analysis which I had the fancy of applying, and have not shown in these classes, as well as the virtuous mean and the excess, the defect also. I do not know that the omission very much matters. Still, as clearness is the one merit which a plain, unsystematic writer, without a philosophy, can hope to have, and as our notion of the three great English classes may perhaps be made clearer if we see their distinctive qualities in the defect, as well as in the excess and in the mean, let us try, before proceeding further, to remedy this omission.

It is manifest, if the perfect and virtuous mean of that fine spirit which is the distinctive quality of aristocracies, is to be found in a high, chivalrous style, and its excess in a fierce turn for resistance, that its defect must lie in a spirit not bold and high enough, and in an excessive and pusillanimous unaptness for resistance. If, again, the perfect and virtuous mean of that force by which our middle class has done its great works, and of that self-reliance with which it contemplates itself and them, is to be seen in the performances and speeches of our commercial member of Parliament, and the excess of that force and of that self-reliance in the performances and speeches of our fanatical Dissenting minister, then it is manifest that their defect must lie in a helpless inaptitude for the great works of the middle class, and in a poor and despicable lack of its self-satisfaction.

To be chosen to exemplify the happy mean of a good quality, or set of good qualities, is evidently a praise to a man; nay, to be chosen to exemplify even their excess, is a kind of praise. Therefore I could have no hesitation in taking actual personages to exemplify, respectively, the mean and the excess of aristocratic and middle-class qualities. But perhaps there might be a want of urbanity in singling out this or that personage as the representative of defect. Therefore I shall leave the defect of aristocracy unillustrated by any representative man. But with oneself one may always, without impropriety, deal quite freely; and, indeed, this sort of plain-dealing with oneself has in it, as all the moralists tell us, something very wholesome. So I will venture to humbly offer myself as an illustration of defect in those forces and qualities which make our middle class what it is. The too well-founded reproaches of my opponents declare how little I have lent a hand to the great works of the middle class; for it is evidently these works, and my slackness at them, which are meant, when I am said to "refuse to lend a hand to the humble operation of uprooting certain definite evils" (such as church-rates and others), and that therefore "the believers in action grow impatient" with me. The line, again, of a still unsatisfied seeker which I have followed, the idea of self-transformation, of growing towards some measure of sweetness and light not yet reached, is evidently at clean variance with the perfect self-satisfaction current in my class, the middle class, and may serve to indicate in me, therefore, the extreme defect of this feeling. But these confessions, though salutary, are bitter and unpleasant.

To pass, then, to the working class. The defect of this class would be the falling short in what Mr. Frederic

Harrison calls those "bright powers of sympathy and ready powers of action," of which we saw in Mr. Odger the virtuous mean, and in Mr. Bradlaugh the excess. The working class is so fast growing and rising at the present time, that instances of this defect cannot well be now very common. Perhaps Canning's "Needy Knife-Grinder" (who is dead, and therefore cannot be pained at my taking him for an illustration) may serve to give us the notion of defect in the essential quality of a working class; or I might even cite (since, though he is alive in the flesh, he is dead to all heed of criticism) my poor old poaching friend, Zephaniah Diggs, who, between his hare-snaring and his gin-drinking, has got his powers of sympathy quite dulled and his powers of action in any great movement of his class hopelessly impaired. But examples of this defect belong, as I have said, to a bygone age rather than to the present.

The same desire for clearness, which has led me thus to extend a little my first analysis of the three great classes of English society, prompts me also to improve my nomenclature for them a little, with a view to making it thereby more manageable. It is awkward and tiresome to be always saying the aristocratic class, the middle class, the working class. For the middle class, for that great body which, as we know, "has done all the great things that have been done in all departments," and which is to be conceived as moving between its two cardinal points of our commercial member of Parliament and our fanatical Protestant Dissenter,—for this class we have a designation which now has become pretty well known, and which we may as well still keep for them, the designation of Philistines. What this term means I have so often explained that I need not repeat it here. For the aristocratic class, conceived mainly as a body moving between the two cardinal points of our chivalrous lord and our defiant baronet, we have as yet got no special designation. Almost all my attention has naturally been concentrated on my own class, the middle class, with which I am in closest sympathy, and which has been, besides, the great power of our day, and has had its praises sung by all speakers and newspapers.

Still the aristocratic class is so important in itself, and the weighty functions which Mr. Carlyle proposes at the present critical time to commit to it, must add so much to its importance, that it seems neglectful, and a strong instance of that want of coherent philosophic method for which Mr. Frederic Harrison blames me, to leave the aristocratic class so much without notice and denomination. It may be thought that the characteristic which I have occasionally mentioned as proper to aristocracies,—their natural inaccessibility, as children of the established fact, to ideas,—points to our extending to this class also the designation of Philistines; the Philistine being, as is well known, the enemy of the children of light or servants of the idea. Nevertheless, there seems to be an inconvenience in thus giving one and the same designation to two very different classes; and besides, if we look into the thing closely, we shall find that the term Philistine conveys a sense which makes it more peculiarly appropriate to our middle class than to our aristocratic. For *Philistine* gives the notion of something particularly stiff-necked and perverse in the resistance to light and its children; and therein it specially suits our middle class, who not only do not pursue sweetness and light, but who even prefer to them that sort of machinery of business, chapels, tea-meetings, and addresses from Mr. Murphy, which makes up the dismal and illiberal life on which I have so often touched. But the aristocratic class has actually, as we have seen, in its well-known politeness, a kind of image or shadow of sweetness; and as for light, if it does not pursue light, it is not that it perversely cherishes some dismal and illiberal existence in preference to light, but it is lured off from following light by those mighty and eternal seducers of our race which weave for this class their most irresistible charms,—by worldly splendour, security, power, and pleasure. These seducers are exterior goods, but in a way they are goods; and he who is hindered by them from caring for light and ideas, is not so much doing what is perverse as what is too natural.

Keeping this in view, I have in my own mind often indulged myself with the fancy of employing, in order to designate our aristocratic class, the name of *The Barbarians*. The Barbarians, to whom we all owe so much, and who reinvigorated and renewed our worn-out Europe, had, as is well known, eminent merits; and in this country, where we are for the most part sprung from the Barbarians, we have never had the prejudice against them which prevails among the races of Latin origin. The Barbarians brought with them that staunch individualism, as the modern phrase is, and that passion for doing as one likes, for the assertion of personal liberty, which appears to Mr. Bright the central idea of English life, and of which we have, at any rate, a very rich supply. The stronghold and natural seat of this passion was in the nobles of whom our aristocratic class are the inheritors; and this class, accordingly, have signally manifested it, and have done much by their example to recommend it to the body of the nation, who already, indeed, had it in their blood. The Barbarians, again, had the passion for field-sports; and they have handed it on to our aristocratic class, who of this passion too, as of the passion for asserting one's personal liberty, are the great natural stronghold. The care of the Barbarians for the body, and for all manly exercises; the vigour, good looks, and fine complexion which they acquired and perpetuated in their families by these means,—all this may be observed still in our aristocratic class. The chivalry of the Barbarians, with its characteristics of high spirit, choice manners, and distinguished bearing,—what is this but the attractive commencement of the politeness of our aristocratic class? In some Barbarian noble, no doubt, one would have admired, if one could have been then alive to see it, the rudiments of our politest peer. Only, all this culture (to call it by that name) of the Barbarians was an exterior culture mainly. It consisted principally in outward gifts and graces, in looks, manners, accomplishments, prowess. The chief inward gifts which had part in it were the most exterior, so to speak, of inward gifts, those which come nearest to outward ones; they were courage, a high spirit, self-confidence. Far within, and unawakened, lay a whole range of powers of thought and feeling, to which these interesting productions of nature had, from the circumstances of their life, no access. Making allowances for the difference of the times, surely we can observe precisely the same thing now in our aristocratic class. In general its culture is exterior chiefly; all the exterior graces and accomplishments, and the more external of the inward virtues, seem to be principally its portion. It now, of course, cannot but be often in contact with those studies by which, from the world of thought and feeling, true culture teaches us to fetch sweetness and light; but its hold upon these very studies appears remarkably external, and unable to exert any deep power upon its spirit. Therefore the one insufficiency which we noted in the perfect mean of this class was an insufficiency of light. And owing to the same causes, does not a subtle criticism lead us to make, even on the good looks and politeness of our aristocratic class, and of even the most fascinating half of that class, the feminine half, the one qualifying remark, that in these charming gifts there should perhaps be, for ideal perfection, a shade more *soul?*

I often, therefore, when I want to distinguish clearly the aristocratic class from the Philistines proper, or middle class, name the former, in my own mind, *the Barbarians.* And when I go through the country, and see this and that beautiful and imposing seat of theirs crowning the landscape, "There," I say to myself, "is a great fortified post of the Barbarians."

It is obvious that that part of the working class which, working diligently by the light of Mrs. Gooch's Golden Rule, looks forward to the happy day when it will sit on thrones with commercial members of Parliament and other middle-class potentates, to survey, as Mr. Bright beautifully says, "the cities it has built, the railroads it has made, the manufactures it has produced, the cargoes which freight the ships of the greatest mercantile navy the world has ever seen,"—it is obvious, I say, that this part of the working class is, or is in a fair way to be, one in spirit with the industrial middle class. It is notorious that our middle-class Liberals have long looked forward to this consummation, when the working class shall join forces with them, aid them heartily to carry forward their great works, go in a body to their tea-meetings, and, in short, enable them to bring about their millennium. That part of the working class, therefore, which does really seem to lend itself to these great aims, may, with propriety, be numbered by us among the Philistines. That part of it, again, which so much occupies the attention of philanthropists at present,—the part which gives all its energies to organising itself, through trades' unions and other means, so as to constitute, first, a great working-class power independent of the middle and

aristocratic classes, and then, by dint of numbers, give
the law to them and itself reign absolutely,—this lively
and promising part must also, according to our definition, go with the Philistines; because it is its class and its
class instinct which it seeks to affirm—its ordinary self,
not its best self; and it is a machinery, an industrial
machinery, and power and pre-eminence and other external goods, which fill its thoughts, and not an inward
perfection. It is wholly occupied, according to Plato's
subtle expression, with the things of itself and not its
real self, with the things of the State and not the real
State. But that vast portion, lastly, of the working class
which, raw and half-developed, has long lain half-hid-
den amidst its poverty and squalor, and is now issuing
from its hiding-place to assert an Englishman's heaven-
born privilege of doing as he likes, and is beginning to
perplex us by marching where it likes, meeting where
it likes, bawling what it likes, breaking what it likes,—
to this vast residuum we may with great propriety give
the name of *Populace*.

Thus we have got three distinct terms, *Barbarians,
Philistines, Populace,* to denote roughly the three great
classes into which our society is divided; and though
this humble attempt at a scientific nomenclature falls,
no doubt, very far short in precision of what might be
required from a writer equipped with a complete and
coherent philosophy, yet, from a notoriously unsystematic and unpretending writer, it will, I trust, be accepted
as sufficient.

But in using this new, and, I hope, convenient division of English society, two things are to be borne in
mind. The first is, that since, under all our class divi-
sions, there is a common basis of human nature, therefore, in every one of us, whether we be properly
Barbarians, Philistines, or Populace, there exists, some-

times only in germ and potentially, sometimes more or
less developed, the same tendencies and passions which
have made our fellow-citizens of other classes what they
are. This consideration is very important, because it has
great influence in begetting that spirit of indulgence
which is a necessary part of sweetness, and which, indeed, when our culture is complete, is, as I have said,
inexhaustible. Thus, an English Barbarian who ex-
amines himself will, in general, find himself to be not so
entirely a Barbarian but that he has in him, also, something of the Philistine, and even something of the Populace as well. And the same with Englishmen of the two
other classes.

This is an experience which we may all verify every
day. For instance, I myself (I again take myself as a sort
of *corpus vile* to serve for illustration in a matter where
serving for illustration may not by every one be thought
agreeable), I myself am properly a Philistine,—Mr.
Swinburne would add, the son of a Philistine. And although, through circumstances which will perhaps one
day be known if ever the affecting history of my con-
version comes to be written, I have, for the most part,
broken with the ideas and the tea-meetings of my own
class, yet I have not, on that account, been brought
much the nearer to the ideas and works of the Barbarians or of the Populace. Nevertheless, I never take a gun
or a fishing-rod in my hands without feeling that I have
in the ground of my nature the self-same seeds which,
fostered by circumstances, do so much to make the Barbarian; and that, with the Barbarian's advantages, I
might have rivalled him. Place me in one of his great
fortified posts, with these seeds of a love for field-sports
sown in my nature, with all the means of developing
them, with all pleasures at my command, with most
whom I met deferring to me, every one I met smiling on

me, and with every appearance of permanence and
security before me and behind me,—then I too might
have grown, I feel, into a very passable child of the
established fact, of commendable spirit and politeness,
and, at the same time, a little inaccessible to ideas and
light; not, of course, with either the eminent fine spirit
of our type of aristocratic perfection, or the eminent turn
for resistance of our type of aristocratic excess, but,
according to the measure of the common run of mankind, something between the two. And as to the Populace, who, whether he be Barbarian or Philistine, can
look at them without sympathy, when he remembers
how often,—every time that we snatch up a vehément
opinion in ignorance and passion, every time that we
long to crush an adversary by sheer violence, every time
that we are envious, every time that we are brutal, every
time that we adore mere power or success, every time
that we add our voice to swell a blind clamour against
some unpopular personage, every time that we trample
savagely on the fallen,—he has found in his own bosom
the eternal spirit of the Populace, and that there needs
only a little help from circumstances to make it triumph
in him untamably.

The second thing to be borne in mind I have in-
dicated several times already. It is this. All of us, so far
as we are Barbarians, Philistines, or Populace, imagine
happiness to consist in doing what one's ordinary self
likes. What one's ordinary self likes differs according to
the class to which one belongs, and has its severer and its
lighter side; always, however, remaining machinery, and
nothing more. The graver self of the Barbarian likes
honours and consideration; his more relaxed self, field-
sports and pleasure. The graver self of one kind of Philistine likes fanaticism, business, and money-making; his
more relaxed self, comfort and tea-meetings. Of another

kind of Philistine, the graver self likes rattening; the
relaxed self, deputations, or hearing Mr. Odger speak.
The sterner self of the Populace likes bawling, hustling,
and smashing; the lighter self, beer. But in each class
there are born a certain number of natures with a curiosity about their best self, with a bent for seeing things
as they are, for disentangling themselves from machinery, for simply concerning themselves with reason and
the will of God, and doing their best to make these prevail;—for the pursuit, in a word, of perfection. To certain manifestations of this love for perfection mankind
have accustomed themselves to give the name of genius;
implying, by this name, something original and heaven-
bestowed in the passion. But the passion is to be found
far beyond those manifestations of it to which the world
usually gives the name of genius, and in which there is,
for the most part, a *talent* of some kind or other, a special and striking faculty of execution, informed by the
heaven-bestowed ardour, or genius. It is to be found in
many manifestations besides these, and may best be
called, as we have called it, the love and pursuit of perfection; culture being the true nurse of the pursuing
love, and sweetness and light the true character of the
pursued perfection. Natures with this bent emerge in all
classes,—among the Barbarians, among the Philistines,
among the Populace. And this bent always tends to take
them out of their class, and to make their distinguish-
ing characteristic not their Barbarianism or their Philistinism, but their *humanity*. They have, in general, a
rough time of it in their lives; but they are sown more
abundantly than one might think, they appear where
and when one least expects it, they set up a fire which
enfilades, so to speak, the class with which they are
ranked; and, in general, by the extrication of their best
self as the self to develop, and by the simplicity of the

ends fixed by them as paramount, they hinder the un-
checked predominance of that class-life which is the
affirmation of our ordinary self, and seasonably discon-
cert mankind in their worship of machinery.

Therefore, when we speak of ourselves as divided into
Barbarians, Philistines, and Populace, we must be understood always to imply that within each of these classes
there are a certain number of *aliens,* if we may so call
them,—persons who are mainly led, not by their class
spirit, but by a general *humane* spirit, by the love of human perfection; and that this number is capable of being
diminished or augmented. I mean, the number of those
who will succeed in developing this happy instinct will
be greater or smaller, in proportion both to the force of
the original instinct within them, and to the hindrance
or encouragement which it meets with from without. In
almost all who have it, it is mixed with some infusion
of the spirit of an ordinary self, some quantity of class-
instinct, and even, as has been shown, of more than one
class-instinct at the same time; so that, in general, the
extrication of the best self, the predominance of the *humane* instinct, will very much depend upon its meeting,
or not, with what is fitted to help and elicit it. At a moment, therefore, when it is agreed that we want a source
of authority, and when it seems probable that the right
source is our best self, it becomes of vast importance to
see whether or not the things around us are, in general,
such as to help and elicit our best self, and if they are
not, to see why they are not, and the most promising
way of mending them.

Now, it is clear that the very absence of any powerful
authority amongst us, and the prevalent doctrine of the
duty and happiness of doing as one likes, and asserting
our personal liberty, must tend to prevent the erection
of any very strict standard of excellence, the belief in

any very paramount authority of right reason, the recognition of our best self as anything very recondite and hard to come at. It may be, as I have said, a proof of our honesty that we do not attempt to give to our ordinary self, as we have it in action, predominant authority, and to impose its rule upon other people. But it is evident also, that it is not easy, with our style of proceeding, to get beyond the notion of an ordinary self at all, or to get the paramount authority of a commanding best self, or right reason, recognised. The learned Martinus Scriblerus well says:—"the taste of the bathos is implanted by nature itself in the soul of man; till, perverted by custom or example, he is taught, or rather compelled, to relish the sublime." But with us everything seems directed to prevent any such perversion of us by custom or example as might compel us to relish the sublime; by all means we are encouraged to keep our natural taste for the bathos unimpaired

I have formerly pointed out how in literature the absence of any authoritative centre, like an Academy, tends to do this. Each section of the public has its own literary organ, and the mass of the public is without any suspicion that the value of these organs is relative to their being nearer a certain ideal centre of correct information, taste, and intelligence, or farther away from it. I have said that within certain limits, which any one who is likely to read this will have no difficulty in drawing for himself, my old adversary, the *Saturday Review*, may, on matters of literature and taste, be fairly enough regarded, relatively to the mass of newspapers which treat these matters, as a kind of organ of reason. But I remember once conversing with a company of Nonconformist admirers of some lecturer who had let off a great firework, which the *Saturday Review* said was all noise and false lights, and feeling my way as tenderly as I could about the effect of this unfavourable judgment upon those with whom I was conversing. "Oh," said one who was their spokesman, with the most tranquil air of conviction, "it is true the *Saturday Review* abuses the lecture, but the *British Banner*" (I am not quite sure it was the *British Banner*, but it was some newspaper of that stamp) "says that the *Saturday Review* is quite wrong." The speaker had evidently no notion that there was a scale of value for judgments on these topics, and that the judgments of the *Saturday Review* ranked high on this scale, and those of the *British Banner* low; the taste of the bathos implanted by nature in the literary judgments of man had never, in my friend's case, encountered any let or hindrance.

Just the same in religion as in literature. We have most of us little idea of a high standard to choose our guides by, of a great and profound spirit which is an authority while inferior spirits are none. It is enough to give importance to things that this or that person says them decisively, and has a large following of some strong kind when he says them. This habit of ours is very well shown in that able and interesting work of Mr. Hepworth Dixon's, which we were all reading lately, *The Mormons, by One of Themselves.* Here, again, I am not quite sure that my memory serves me as to the exact title, but I mean the well-known book in which Mr. Hepworth Dixon described the Mormons, and other similar religious bodies in America, with so much detail and such warm sympathy. In this work it seems enough for Mr. Dixon that this or that doctrine has its Rabbi, who talks big to him, has a staunch body of disciples, and, above all, has plenty of rifles. That there are any further stricter tests to be applied to a doctrine, before it is pronounced important, never seems to occur to him. "It is easy to say," he writes of the Mormons, "that these saints are dupes and fanatics, to laugh at Joe Smith and his church, but what then? *The great facts remain.* Young and his people are at Utah; a church of 200,000 souls; an army of 20,000 rifles." But if the followers of a doctrine are really dupes, or worse, and its promulgators are really fanatics, or worse, it gives the doctrine no seriousness or authority the more that there should be found 200,000 souls,—200,000 of the innumerable multitude with a natural taste for the bathos,—to hold it, and 20,000 rifles to defend it. And again, of another religious organisation in America: "A fair and open field is not to be refused when hosts so mighty throw down wager of battle on behalf of what they hold to be true, however strange their faith may seem." A fair and open field is not to be refused to any speaker; but this solemn way of heralding him is quite out of place, unless he has, for the best reason and spirit of man, some significance. "Well, but," says Mr. Hepworth Dixon, "a theory which has been accepted by men like Judge Edmonds, Dr. Hare, Elder Frederick, and Professor Bush!" And again: "Such are, in brief, the bases of what Newman Weeks, Sarah Horton, Deborah Butler, and the associated brethren, proclaimed in Rolt's Hall as the new covenant!" If he was summing up an account of the doctrine of Plato, or of St. Paul, and of its followers, Mr. Hepworth Dixon could not be more earnestly reverential. But the question is, Have personages like Judge Edmonds, and Newman Weeks, and Elderess Polly, and Elderess Antoinette, and the rest of Mr. Hepworth Dixon's heroes and heroines, anything of the weight and significance for the best reason and spirit of man that Plato and St. Paul have? Evidently they, at present, have not; and a very small taste of them and their doctrines ought to have convinced Mr. Hepworth Dixon that they never could have. "But," says he, "the magnetic power which Shakerism is exercising on American thought would of itself compel us,"—and so on. Now, so far as real thought is concerned,—thought which affects the best reason and spirit of man, the scientific or the imaginative thought of the world, the only thought which deserves speaking of in this solemn way, —America has up to the present time been hardly more than a province of England, and even now would not herself claim to be more than abreast of England; and of this only real human thought, English thought itself is not just now, as we must all admit, the most signifi-cant factor. Neither, then, can American thought be; and the magnetic power which Shakerism exercises on Amer-ican thought is about as important, for the best reason and spirit of man, as the magnetic power which Mr. Murphy exercises on Birmingham Protestantism. And as we shall never get rid of our natural taste for the bathos in religion,—never get access to a best self and right reason which may stand as a serious authority,—by treating Mr. Murphy as his own disciples treat him, seriously, and as if he was as much an authority as any one else: so we shall never get rid of it while our able and popular writers treat their Joe Smiths and Deborah Butlers, with their so many thousand souls and so many thousand rifles, in the like exaggerated and misleading manner, and so do their best to confirm us in a bad men-tal habit to which we are already too prone.

If our habits make it hard for us to come at the idea of a high best self, of a paramount authority, in litera-ture or religion, how much more do they make this hard in the sphere of politics! In other countries the gover-nors, not depending so immediately on the favour of the governed, have everything to urge them, if they know anything of right reason (and it is at least supposed that governors should know more of this than the mass of the governed), to set it authoritatively before the community. But our whole scheme of government being representative, every one of our governors has all possible temptation, instead of setting up before the governed who elect him, and on whose favour he depends, a high standard of right reason, to accommodate himself as much as possible to their natural taste for the bathos; and even if he tries to go counter to it, to proceed in this with so much flattering and coaxing, that they shall not suspect their ignorance and prejudices to be anything very unlike right reason, or their natural taste for the bathos to differ much from a relish for the sublime. Every one is thus in every possible way encouraged to trust in his own heart; but, "he that trusteth in his own heart," says the Wise Man, "is a fool"; and at any rate this, which Bishop Wilson says, is undeniably true: "The number of those who need to be awakened is far greater than that of those who need comfort."

But in our political system everybody is comforted. Our guides and governors who have to be elected by the influence of the Barbarians, and who depend on their favour, sing the praises of the Barbarians, and say all the smooth things that can be said of them. With Mr. Tennyson, they celebrate "the great broad-shoul-dered genial Englishman," with his "sense of duty," his "reverence for the laws," and his "patient force," who saves us from the "revolts, republics, revolutions, most no graver than a schoolboy's barring out," which upset other and less broad-shouldered nations. Our guides who are chosen by the Philistines and who have to look to their favour, tell the Philistines how "all the world knows that the great middle class of this country supplies the mind, the will, and the power requisite for all the great and good things that have to be done," and congratulate them on their "earnest good sense, which penetrates through sophisms, ignores commonplaces, and gives to conventional illusions their true value." Our guides who look to the favour of the Populace, tell them that "theirs are the brightest powers of sympathy, and the readiest powers of action."

Harsh things are said too, no doubt, against all the great classes of the community; but these things so evidently come from a hostile class, and are so manifestly dictated by the passions and prepossessions of a hostile class, and not by right reason, that they make no serious impression on those at whom they are launched, but slide easily off their minds. For instance, when the Reform League orators inveigh against our cruel and bloated aristocracy, these invectives so evidently show the passions and point of view of the Populace, that they do not sink into the minds of those at whom they are addressed, or awaken any thought or self-examination in them. Again, when our aristocratical baronet describes the Philistines and the Populace as influenced with a kind of hideous mania for emasculating the aristocracy, that reproach so clearly comes from the wrath and excited imagination of the Barbarians, that it does not much set the Philistines and the Populace thinking. Or when Mr. Lowe calls the Populace drunken and venal, he so evidently calls them this in an agony of apprehension for his Philistine or middle-class Parliament, which has done so many great and heroic works, and is now threatened with mixture and debasement, that the Populace do not lay his words seriously to heart.

So the voice which makes a permanent impression on each of our classes is the voice of its friends, and this is from the nature of things, as I have said, a comforting voice. The Barbarians remain in the belief that the great broad-shouldered genial Englishman may be well satisfied with himself; the Philistines remain in the belief

that the great middle class of this country, with its earnest common-sense penetrating through sophisms and
ignoring commonplaces, may be well satisfied with itself; the Populace, that the working man with his bright
powers of sympathy and ready powers of action, may
be well satisfied with himself. What hope, at this rate,
of extinguishing the taste of the bathos implanted by
nature itself in the soul of man, or of inculcating the
belief that excellence dwells among high and steep
rocks, and can only be reached by those who sweat
blood to reach her?

But it will be said, perhaps, that candidates for political influence and leadership, who thus caress the self-
love of those whose suffrages they desire, know quite
well that they are not saying the sheer truth as reason
sees it, but that they are using a sort of conventional
language, or what we call clap-trap, which is essential
to the working of representative institutions. And therefore, I suppose, we ought rather to say with Figaro: *Qui
est-ce qu'on trompe ici?* Now, I admit that often, but
not always, when our governors say smooth things to the
self-love of the class whose political support they want,
they know very well that they are overstepping, by a
long stride, the bounds of truth and soberness; and
while they talk, they in a manner, no doubt, put their
tongue in their cheek. Not always; because, when a
Barbarian appeals to his own class to make him their
representative and give him political power, he, when
he pleases their self-love by extolling broad-shouldered
genial Englishmen with their sense of duty, reverence
for the laws, and patient force, pleases his own self-love
and extols himself, and is, therefore, himself ensnared by
his own smooth words. And so, too, when a Philistine
wants to be sent to Parliament by his brother Philistines,
and extols the earnest good sense which characterises

Manchester and supplies the mind, the will, and the power, as the *Daily News* eloquently says, requisite for all the great and good things that have to be done, he intoxicates and deludes himself as well as his brother Philistines who hear him.

But it is true that a Barbarian often wants the political support of the Philistines; and he unquestionably, when he flatters the self-love of Philistinism, and extols, in the approved fashion, its energy, enterprise, and self-reliance, knows that he is talking clap-trap, and so to say, puts his tongue in his cheek. On all matters where Nonconformity and its catchwords are concerned, this insincerity of Barbarians needing Nonconformist support, and, therefore, flattering the self-love of Nonconformity and repeating its catchwords without the least real belief in them, is very noticeable. When the Nonconformists, in a transport of blind zeal, threw out Sir James Graham's useful Education Clauses in 1843, one-half of their Parliamentary advocates, no doubt, who cried aloud against "trampling on the religious liberty of the Dissenters by taking the money of Dissenters to teach the tenets of the Church of England," put their tongue in their cheek while they so cried out. And perhaps there is even a sort of motion of Mr. Frederic Harrison's tongue towards his cheek when he talks of "the shriek of superstition," and tells the working class that "theirs are the brightest powers of sympathy and the readiest powers of action." But the point on which I would insist is, that this involuntary tribute to truth and soberness on the part of certain of our governors and guides never reaches at all the mass of us governed, to serve as a lesson to us, to abate our self-love, and to awaken in us a suspicion that our favourite prejudices may be, to a higher reason, all nonsense. Whatever by-play goes on among the more intelligent of our leaders, we do not see it; and we are left to believe that, not only in our own eyes, but in the eyes of our representative and ruling men, there is nothing more admirable than our ordinary self, whatever our ordinary self happens to be, Barbarian, Philistine, or Populace.

Thus everything in our political life tends to hide from us that there is anything wiser than our ordinary selves, and to prevent our getting the notion of a paramount right reason. Royalty itself, in its idea the expression of the collective nation, and a sort of constituted witness to its best mind, we try to turn into a kind of grand advertising van, meant to give publicity and credit to the inventions, sound or unsound, of the ordinary self of individuals.

I remember, when I was in North Germany, having this very strongly brought to my mind in the matter of schools and their institution. In Prussia, the best schools are Crown patronage schools, as they are called; schools which have been established and endowed (and new ones are to this day being established and endowed) by the Sovereign himself out of his own revenues, to be under the direct control and management of him or of those representing him, and to serve as types of what schools should be. The Sovereign, as his position raises him above many prejudices and littlenesses, and as he can always have at his disposal the best advice, has evident advantages over private founders in well planning and directing a school; while at the same time his great means and his great influence secure, to a well-planned school of his, credit and authority. This is what, in North Germany, the governors do in the matter of education for the governed; and one may say that they thus give the governed a lesson, and draw out in them the idea of a right reason higher than the suggestions of an ordinary man's ordinary self.

But in England how different is the part which in this matter our governors are accustomed to play! The Licensed Victuallers or the Commercial Travellers propose to make a school for their children; and I suppose, in the matter of schools, one may call the Licensed Victuallers or the Commercial Travellers ordinary men, with their natural taste for the bathos still strong; and a Sovereign with the advice of men like Wilhelm von Humboldt or Schleiermacher may, in this matter, be a better judge, and nearer to right reason. And it will be allowed, probably, that right reason would suggest that, to have a sheer school of Licensed Victuallers' children, or a sheer school of Commercial Travellers' children, and to bring them all up, not only at home but at school too, in a kind of odour of licensed victualism or of bagmanism, is not a wise training to give to these children. And in Germany, I have said, the action of the national guides or governors is to suggest and provide a better. But, in England, the action of the national guides or governors is, for a Royal Prince or a great Minister to go down to the opening of the Licensed Victuallers' or of the Commercial Travellers' school, to take the chair, to extol the energy and self-reliance of the Licensed Victuallers or the Commercial Travellers, to be all of their way of thinking, to predict full success to their schools, and never so much as to hint to them that they are probably doing a very foolish thing, and that the right way to go to work with their children's education is quite different. And it is the same in almost every department of affairs. While, on the Continent, the idea prevails that it is the business of the heads and representatives of the nation, by virtue of their superior means, power, and information, to set an example and to provide suggestions of right reason, among us the idea is that the business of the heads and representatives of the nation is to do nothing of the kind, but to applaud the natural taste for the bathos showing itself vigorously in any part of the community, and to encourage its works.

Now I do not say that the political system of foreign countries has not inconveniences which may outweigh the inconveniences of our own political system; nor am I the least proposing to get rid of our own political system and to adopt theirs. But a sound centre of authority being what, in this disquisition, we have been led to seek, and right reason, or our best self, appearing alone to offer such a sound centre of authority, it is necessary to take note of the chief impediments which hinder, in this country, the extrication or recognition of this right reason as a paramount authority, with a view to afterwards trying in what way they can best be removed.

This being borne in mind, I proceed to remark how not only do we get no suggestions of right reason, and no rebukes of our ordinary self, from our governors, but a kind of philosophical theory is widely spread among us to the effect that there is no such thing at all as a best self and a right reason having claim to paramount authority, or, at any rate, no such thing ascertainable and capable of being made use of; and that there is nothing but an infinite number of ideas and works of our ordinary selves, and suggestions of our natural taste for the bathos, pretty nearly equal in value, which are doomed either to an irreconcilable conflict, or else to a perpetual give and take; and that wisdom consists in choosing the give and take rather than the conflict, and in sticking to our choice with patience and good humour.

And, on the other hand, we have another philosophical theory rife among us, to the effect that without the labour of perverting ourselves by custom or example to relish right reason, but by continuing all of us to follow freely our natural taste for the bathos, we shall, by the mercy of Providence, and by a kind of natural tendency of things, come in due time to relish and follow right reason.

The great promoters of these philosophical theories are our newspapers, which, no less than our parliamentary representatives, may be said to act the part of guides and governors to us; and these favourite doctrines of theirs I call,—or should call, if the doctrines were not preached by authorities I so much respect,—the first, a peculiarly British form of Atheism, the second, a peculiarly British form of Quietism. The first-named melancholy doctrine is preached in the *Times* with great clearness and force of style; indeed, it is well known, from the example of the poet Lucretius and others, what great masters of style the atheistic doctrine has always counted among its promulgators. "It is of no use," says the *Times*, "for us to attempt to force upon our neighbours our several likings and dislikings. We must take things as they are. Everybody has his own little vision of religious or civil perfection. Under the evident impossibility of satisfying everybody, we agree to take our stand on equal laws and on a system as open and liberal as is possible. The result is that everybody has more liberty of action and of speaking here than anywhere else in the Old World." We come again here upon Mr. Roebuck's celebrated definition of happiness, on which I have so often commented: "I look around me and ask what is the state of England? Is not every man able to say what he likes? I ask you whether the world over, or in past history, there is anything like it? Nothing. I pray that our unrivalled happiness may last." This is the old story of our system of checks and every

Englishman doing as he likes, which we have already seen to have been convenient enough so long as there were only the Barbarians and the Philistines to do what they liked, but to be getting inconvenient, and productive of anarchy, now that the Populace wants to do what it likes too.

But for all that, I will not at once dismiss this famous doctrine, but will first quote another passage from the *Times*, applying the doctrine to a matter of which we have just been speaking,—education. "The difficulty here" (in providing a national system of education), says the *Times*, "does not reside in any removable arrangements. It is inherent and native in the actual and inveterate state of things in this country. All these powers and personages, all these conflicting influences and varieties of character, exist, and have long existed among us; they are fighting it out, and will long continue to fight it out, without coming to that happy consummation when some one element of the British character is to destroy or to absorb all the rest." There it is! the various promptings of the natural taste for the bathos in this man and that amongst us are fighting it out; and the day will never come (and, indeed, why should we wish it to come?) when one man's particular sort of taste for the bathos shall tyrannise over another man's; nor when right reason (if that may be called an element of the British character) shall absorb and rule them all. "The whole system of this country, like the constitution we boast to inherit, and are glad to uphold, is made up of established facts, prescriptive authorities, existing usages, powers that be, persons in possession, and communities or classes that have won dominion for themselves, and will hold it against all comers." Every force in the world, evidently, except the one reconciling force, right reason! Barbarian here, Philistine there, Mr. Bradlaugh and

Populace striking in!—pull devil, pull baker! Really,
presented with the mastery of style of our leading
journal, the sad picture, as one gazes upon it, assumes
the iron and inexorable solemnity of tragic Destiny.

After this, the milder doctrine of our other philosophical teacher, the *Daily News*, has, at first, something
very attractive and assuaging. The *Daily News* begins,
indeed, in appearance, to weave the iron web of necessity round us like the *Times*. "The alternative is between
a man's doing what he likes and his doing what some
one else, probably not one whit wiser than himself,
likes." This points to the tacit compact, mentioned in
my last paper, between the Barbarians and the Philistines, and into which it is hoped that the Populace will
one day enter; the compact, so creditable to English
honesty, that since each class has only the ideas and aims
of its ordinary self to give effect to, none of them shall, if
it exercise power, treat its ordinary self too seriously, or
attempt to impose it on others; but shall let these others,
—the fanatical Protestant, for instance, in his Papist-
baiting, and the popular tribune in his Hyde Park an-
archy-mongering,—have their fling. But then the *Daily
News* suddenly lights up the gloom of necessitarianism
with bright beams of hope. "No doubt," it says, "the
common reason of society ought to check the aberrations
of individual eccentricity." This common reason of society looks very like our best self or right reason, to
which we want to give authority, by making the action
of the *State*, or nation in its collective character, the
expression of it. But of this project of ours, the *Daily
News*, with its subtle dialectics, makes havoc. "Make
the State the organ of the common reason?"—it says.
"You make it the organ of something or other, but how
can you be certain that reason will be the quality which
will be embodied in it?" You cannot be certain of it, un-

doubtedly, if you never try to bring the thing about; but the question is, the action of the State being the action of the collective nation, and the action of the collective nation carrying naturally great publicity, weight, and force of example with it, whether we should not try to put into the action of the State as much as possible of right reason or our best self, which may, in this manner, come back to us with new force and authority; may have visibility, form, and influence; and help to confirm us, in the many moments when we are tempted to be our ordinary selves merely, in resisting our natural taste of the bathos rather than in giving way to it?

But no! says our teacher: "It is better there should be an infinite variety of experiments in human action; the common reason of society will in the main check the aberrations of individual eccentricity well enough, if left to its natural operation." This is what I call the specially British form of Quietism, or a devout, but excessive reliance on an over-ruling Providence. Providence, as the moralists are careful to tell us, generally works in human affairs by human means; so, when we want to make right reason act on individual inclination, our best self on our ordinary self, we seek to give it more power of doing so by giving it public recognition and authority, and embodying it, so far as we can, in the State. It seems too much to ask of Providence, that while we, on our part, leave our congenital taste for the bathos to its natural operation and its infinite variety of experiments, Providence should mysteriously guide it into the true track, and compel it to relish the sublime. At any rate, great men and great institutions have hitherto seemed necessary for producing any considerable effect of this kind. No doubt we have an infinite variety of experiments and an ever-multiplying multitude of explorers. Even in these few chapters I have enumerated many:

the *British Banner*, Judge Edmonds, Newman Weeks,
Deborah Butler, Elderess Polly, Brother Noyes, Mr.
Murphy, the Licensed Victuallers, the Commercial
Travellers, and I know not how many more; and the
members of the noble army are swelling every day. But
what a depth of Quietism, or rather, what an over-
bold call on the direct interposition of Providence, to
believe that these interesting explorers will discover
the true track, or at any rate, "will do so in the main
well enough" (whatever that may mean) if left to
their natural operation; that is, by going on as they
are! Philosophers say, indeed, that we learn virtue by
performing acts of virtue; but to say that we shall learn
virtue by performing any acts to which our natural
taste for the bathos carries us, that the fanatical Protestant comes at his best self by Papist-baiting, or
Newman Weeks and Deborah Butler at right reason by
following their noses, this certainly does appear over-
sanguine.

It is true, what we want is to make right reason act
on individual reason, the reason of individuals; all our
search for authority has that for its end and aim. The
Daily News says, I observe, that all my argument for
authority "has a non-intellectual root"; and from what I
know of my own mind and its poverty I think this so
probable, that I should be inclined easily to admit it,
if it were not that, in the first place, nothing of this
kind, perhaps, should be admitted without examination;
and, in the second, a way of accounting for the charge being made, in this particular instance, without good
grounds, appears to present itself. What seems to me to
account here, perhaps, for the charge, is the want of flexibility of our race, on which I have so often remarked. I
mean, it being admitted that the conformity of the individual reason of the fanatical Protestant or the popular

rioter with right reason is our true object, and not the
mere restraining them, by the strong arm of the State,
from Papist-baiting, or railing-breaking,—admitting this,
we English have so little flexibility that we cannot readily
perceive that the State's restraining them from these indulgences may yet fix clearly in their minds that, to the
collective nation, these indulgences appear irrational
and unallowable, may make them pause and reflect, and
may contribute to bringing, with time, their individual
reason into harmony with right reason. But in no country, owing to the want of intellectual flexibility above
mentioned, is the leaning which is our natural one, and,
therefore, needs no recommending to us, so sedulously
recommended, and the leaning which is not our natural
one, and, therefore, does not need dispraising to us, so
sedulously dispraised, as in ours. To rely on the individual being, with us, the natural leaning, we will
hear of nothing but the good of relying on the individual; to act through the collective nation on the
individual being not our natural leaning, we will hear
nothing in recommendation of it. But the wise know
that we often need to hear most of that to which we are
least inclined, and even to learn to employ, in certain
circumstances, that which is capable, if employed amiss,
of being a danger to us.

Elsewhere this is certainly better understood than
here. In a recent number of the *Westminster Review*,
an able writer, but with precisely our national want of
flexibility of which I have been speaking, has unearthed,
I see, for our present needs, an English translation,
published some years ago, of Wilhelm von Humboldt's
book, *The Sphere and Duties of Government.* Humboldt's object in this book is to show that the operation
of government ought to be severely limited to what
directly and immediately relates to the security of per-

son and property. Wilhelm von Humboldt, one of the
most beautiful souls that have ever existed, used to say
that one's business in life was first to perfect one's self
by all the means in one's power, and secondly, to try
and create in the world around one an aristocracy, the
most numerous that one possibly could, of talents and
characters. He saw, of course, that, in the end, everything comes to this,—that the individual must act for
himself, and must be perfect in himself; and he lived in
a country, Germany, where people were disposed to act
too little for themselves, and to rely too much on the
Government. But even thus, such was his flexibility, so
little was he in bondage to a mere abstract maxim, that
he saw very well that for his purpose itself, of enabling
the individual to stand perfect on his own foundations
and to do without the State, the action of the State
would for long, long years be necessary. And soon after
he wrote his book on *The Sphere and Duties of Government*, Wilhelm von Humboldt became Minister of
Education in Prussia; and from his ministry all the
great reforms which give the control of Prussian education to the State,—the transference of the management
of public schools from their old boards of trustees to the
State, the obligatory State-examination for schoolmasters,
and the foundation of the great State-University of
Berlin,—take their origin. This his English reviewer
says not a word of. But, writing for a people whose
dangers lie, as we have seen, on the side of their un-
checked and unguided individual action, whose dangers
none of them lie on the side of an over-reliance on the
State, he quotes just so much of Wilhelm von Humboldt's
example as can flatter them in their propensities, and do
them no good; and just what might make them think,
and be of use to them, he leaves on one side. This
precisely recalls the manner, it will be observed, in

which we have seen that our royal and noble personages proceed with the Licensed Victuallers.

In France the action of the State on individuals is yet more preponderant than in Germany; and the need which friends of human perfection feel for what may enable the individual to stand perfect on his own foundations is all the stronger. But what says one of the staunchest of these friends, M. Renan, on State action; and even State action in that very sphere where in France it is most excessive, the sphere of education? Here are his words:—"A Liberal believes in liberty, and liberty signifies the non-intervention of the State. *But such an ideal is still a long way off from us, and the very means to remove it to an indefinite distance would be precisely the State's withdrawing its action too soon.*" And this, he adds, is even truer of education than of any other department of public affairs.

We see, then, how indispensable to that human perfection which we seek is, in the opinion of good judges, some public recognition and establishment of our best self, or right reason. We see how our habits and practice oppose themselves to such a recognition, and the many inconveniences which we therefore suffer. But now let us try to go a little deeper, and to find, beneath our actual habits and practice, the very ground and cause out of which they spring.

IV. HEBRAISM AND HELLENISM

This fundamental ground is our preference of doing to thinking. Now this preference is a main element in our nature, and as we study it we find ourselves opening up a number of large questions on every side.

Let me go back for a moment to Bishop Wilson, who says: "First, never go against the best light you have;

secondly, take care that your light be not darkness." We show, as a nation, laudable energy and persistence in walking according to the best light we have, but are not quite careful enough, perhaps, to see that our light be not darkness. This is only another version of the old story that energy is our strong point and favourable characteristic, rather than intelligence. But we may give to this idea a more general form still, in which it will have a yet larger range of application. We may regard this energy driving at practice, this paramount sense of the obligation of duty, self-control, and work, this earnestness in going manfully with the best light we have, as one force. And we may regard the intelligence driving at those ideas which are, after all, the basis of right practice, the ardent sense for all the new and changing combinations of them which man's development brings with it, the indomitable impulse to know and adjust them perfectly, as another force. And these two forces we may regard as in some sense rivals,—rivals not by the necessity of their own nature, but as exhibited in man and his history,—and rivals dividing the empire of the world between them. And to give these forces names from the two races of men who have supplied the most signal and splendid manifestations of them, we may call them respectively the forces of Hebraism and Hellenism. Hebraism and Hellenism,—between these two points of influence moves our world. At one time it feels more powerfully the attraction of one of them, at another time of the other; and it ought to be, though it never is, evenly and happily balanced between them.

The final aim of both Hellenism and Hebraism, as of all great spiritual disciplines, is no doubt the same: man's perfection or salvation. The very language which they both of them use in schooling us to reach this aim is often identical. Even when their language indicates by variation,—sometimes a broad variation, often a but slight and subtle variation,—the different courses of thought which are uppermost in each discipline, even then the unity of the final end and aim is still apparent. To employ the actual words of that discipline with which we ourselves are all of us most familiar, and the words of which, therefore, come most home to us, that final end and aim is "that we might be partakers of the divine nature." These are the words of a Hebrew apostle, but of Hellenism and Hebraism alike this is, I say, the aim. When the two are confronted, as they very often are confronted, it is nearly always with what I may call a rhetorical purpose; the speaker's whole design is to exalt and enthrone one of the two, and he uses the other only as a foil and to enable him the better to give effect to his purpose. Obviously, with us, it is usually Hellenism which is thus reduced to minister to the triumph of Hebraism. There is a sermon on Greece and the Greek spirit by a man never to be mentioned without interest and respect, Frederick Robertson, in which this rhetorical use of Greece and the Greek spirit, and the inadequate exhibition of them necessarily consequent upon this, is almost ludicrous, and would be censurable if it were not to be explained by the exigencies of a sermon. On the other hand, Heinrich Heine, and other writers of his sort, give us the spectacle of the tables completely turned, and of Hebraism brought in just as a foil and contrast to Hellenism, and to make the superiority of Hellenism more manifest. In both these cases there is injustice and misrepresentation. The aim and end of both Hebraism and Hellenism is, as I have said, one and the same, and this aim and end is august and admirable.

Still, they pursue this aim by very different courses. The uppermost idea with Hellenism is to see things as they really are; the uppermost idea with Hebraism is

conduct and obedience. Nothing can do away with this
ineffaceable difference. The Greek quarrel with the
body and its desires is, that they hinder right thinking;
the Hebrew quarrel with them is, that they hinder right
acting. "He that keepeth the law, happy is he"; "Blessed
is the man that feareth the Eternal, that delighteth
greatly in his commandments";—that is the Hebrew
notion of felicity; and, pursued with passion and tenacity, this notion would not let the Hebrew rest till,
as is well known, he had at last got out of the law a network of prescriptions to enwrap his whole life, to govern
every moment of it, every impulse, every action. The
Greek notion of felicity, on the other hand, is perfectly
conveyed in these words of a great French moralist:
"*C'est le bonheur des hommes,*"—when? when they
abhor that which is evil?—no; when they exercise themselves in the law of the Lord day and night?—no; when
they die daily?—no; when they walk about the New
Jerusalem with palms in their hands?—no; but when
they think aright, when their thought hits: "*quand ils
pensent juste.*" At the bottom of both the Greek and
the Hebrew notion is the desire, native in man, for reason and the will of God, the feeling after the universal
order,—in a word, the love of God. But, while Hebraism
seizes upon certain plain, capital intimations of the
universal order, and rivets itself, one may say, with
unequalled grandeur of earnestness and intensity on the
study and observance of them, the bent of Hellenism
is to follow, with flexible activity, the whole play of the
universal order, to be apprehensive of missing any part
of it, of sacrificing one part to another, to slip away from
resting in this or that intimation of it, however capital.
An unclouded clearness of mind, an unimpeded play of
thought, is what this bent drives at. The governing idea

of Hellenism is *spontaneity of consciousness*; that of Hebraism, *strictness of conscience*.

Christianity changed nothing in this essential bent of Hebraism to set doing above knowing. Self-conquest, self-devotion, the following not our own individual will, but the will of God, *obedience*, is the fundamental idea of this form, also, of the discipline to which we have attached the general name of Hebraism. Only, as the old law and the network of prescriptions with which it enveloped human life were evidently a motive-power not driving and searching enough to produce the result aimed at,—patient continuance in well-doing, self-conquest,—Christianity substituted for them boundless devotion to that inspiring and affecting pattern of self-conquest offered by Jesus Christ; and by the new motive-power, of which the essence was this, though the love and admiration of Christian churches have for centuries been employed in varying, amplifying, and adorning the plain description of it, Christianity, as St. Paul truly says, "establishes the law," and in the strength of the ampler power which she has thus supplied to fulfil it, has accomplished the miracles, which we all see, of her history.

So long as we do not forget that both Hellenism and Hebraism are profound and admirable manifestations of man's life, tendencies, and powers, and that both of them aim at a like final result, we can hardly insist too strongly on the divergence of line and of operation with which they proceed. It is a divergence so great that it most truly, as the prophet Zechariah says, "has raised up thy sons, O Zion, against thy sons, O Greece!" The difference whether it is by doing or by knowing that we set most store, and the practical consequences which follow from this difference, leave their

mark on all the history of our race and of its development. Language may be abundantly quoted from both
Hellenism and Hebraism to make it seem that one follows the same current as the other towards the same
goal. They are, truly, borne towards the same goal; but
the currents which bear them are infinitely different. It
is true, Solomon will praise knowing: "Understanding
is a well-spring of life unto him that hath it." And in
the New Testament, again, Jesus Christ is a "light," and
"truth makes us free." It is true, Aristotle will under-
value knowing: "In what concerns virtue," says he,
"three things are necessary—knowledge, deliberate will,
and perseverance; but, whereas the two last are all-im-
portant, the first is a matter of little importance." It is
true that with the same impatience with which St. James
enjoins a man to be not a forgetful hearer, but a *doer of
the work*, Epictetus exhorts us to *do* what we have dem-
onstrated to ourselves we ought to do; or he taunts us
with futility, for being armed at all points to prove that
lying is wrong, yet all the time continuing to lie. It is
true, Plato, in words which are almost the words of the
New Testament or the Imitation, calls life a learning to
die. But underneath the superficial agreement the fundamental divergence still subsists. The understanding of
Solomon is "the walking in the way of the commandments"; this is "the way of peace," and it is of this that
blessedness comes. In the New Testament, the truth
which gives us the peace of God and makes us free, is
the love of Christ constraining us to crucify, as he did,
and with a like purpose of moral regeneration, the flesh
with its affections and lusts, and thus establishing, as we
have seen, the law. The moral virtues, on the other
hand, are with Aristotle but the porch and access to the
intellectual, and with these last is blessedness. That
partaking of the divine life, which both Hellenism and

Hebraism, as we have said, fix as their crowning aim, Plato expressly denies to the man of practical virtue merely, of self-conquest with any other motive than that of perfect intellectual vision. He reserves it for the lover of pure knowledge, of seeing things as they really are, —the φιλομαθής.

Both Hellenism and Hebraism arise out of the wants of human nature, and address themselves to satisfying those wants. But their methods are so different, they lay stress on such different points, and call into being by their respective disciplines such different activities, that the face which human nature presents when it passes from the hands of one of them to those of the other, is no longer the same. To get rid of one's ignorance, to see things as they are, and by seeing them as they are to see them in their beauty, is the simple and attractive ideal which Hellenism holds out before human nature; and from the simplicity and charm of this ideal, Hellenism, and human life in the hands of Hellenism, is invested with a kind of aërial ease, clearness, and radiancy; they are full of what we call sweetness and light. Difficulties are kept out of view, and the beauty and rationalness of the ideal have all our thoughts. "The best man is he who most tries to perfect himself, and the happiest man is he who most feels that he *is* perfecting himself,"—this account of the matter by Socrates, the true Socrates of the *Memorabilia*, has something so simple, spontaneous, and unsophisticated about it, that it seems to fill us with clearness and hope when we hear it. But there is a saying which I have heard attributed to Mr. Carlyle about Socrates,—a very happy saying, whether it is really Mr. Carlyle's or not,—which excellently marks the essential point in which Hebraism differs from Hellenism. "Socrates," this saying goes, "is terribly *at ease in Zion*." Hebraism,—and here is the source of its wonderful strength,—has always been severely preoccupied with an awful sense of the impossibility of being at ease in Zion; of the difficulties which oppose themselves to man's pursuit or attainment of that perfection of which Socrates talks so hopefully, and, as from this point of view one might almost say, so glibly. It is all very well to talk of getting rid of one's ignorance, of seeing things in their reality, seeing them in their beauty; but how is this to be done when there is something which thwarts and spoils all our efforts?

This something is *sin*; and the space which sin fills in Hebraism, as compared with Hellenism, is indeed prodigious. This obstacle to perfection fills the whole scene, and perfection appears remote and rising away from earth, in the background. Under the name of sin, the difficulties of knowing oneself and conquering oneself which impede man's passage to perfection, become, for Hebraism, a positive, active entity hostile to man, a mysterious power which I heard Dr. Pusey the other day, in one of his impressive sermons, compare to a hideous hunchback seated on our shoulders, and which it is the main business of our lives to hate and oppose. The discipline of the Old Testament may be summed up as a discipline teaching us to abhor and flee from sin; the discipline of the New Testament, as a discipline teaching us to die to it. As Hellenism speaks of thinking clearly, seeing things in their essence and beauty, as a grand and precious feat for man to achieve, so Hebraism speaks of becoming conscious of sin, of awakening to a sense of sin, as a feat of this kind. It is obvious to what wide divergence these differing tendencies, actively followed, must lead. As one passes and repasses from Hellenism to Hebraism, from Plato to St. Paul, one feels inclined to rub one's eyes and ask oneself whether man is indeed a gentle and simple being, showing the traces of a noble and divine nature; or an unhappy chained captive, labouring with groanings that cannot be uttered to free himself from the body of this death.

Apparently it was the Hellenic conception of human nature which was unsound, for the world could not live by it. Absolutely to call it unsound, however, is to fall into the common error of its Hebraising enemies; but it was unsound at that particular moment of man's development, it was premature. The indispensable basis of conduct and self-control, the platform upon which alone the perfection aimed at by Greece can come into bloom, was not to be reached by our race so easily; centuries of probation and discipline were needed to bring us to it. Therefore the bright promise of Hellenism faded, and Hebraism ruled the world. Then was seen that astonishing spectacle, so well marked by the often-quoted words of the prophet Zechariah, when men of all languages and nations took hold of the skirt of him that was a Jew, saying:—"*We will go with you, for we have heard that God is with you.*" And the Hebraism which thus received and ruled a world all gone out of the way and altogether become unprofitable, was, and could not but be, the later, the more spiritual, the more attractive development of Hebraism. It was Christianity; that is to say, Hebraism aiming at self-conquest and rescue from the thrall of vile affections, not by obedience to the letter of a law, but by conformity to the image of a self-sacrificing example. To a world stricken with moral enervation Christianity offered its spectacle of an inspired self-sacrifice; to men who refused themselves nothing, it showed one who refused himself everything;—"*my Saviour banished joy!*" says George Herbert. When the *alma Venus*, the life-giving and joy-giving power of nature, so fondly cherished by the Pagan world, could not save her followers from self-dissatisfaction and ennui, the severe words of the apostle came bracingly and refreshingly: "Let no man deceive you with vain words, for because of these things cometh the wrath of God upon the children of disobedience." Through age after age and generation after generation, our race, or all that part of our race which was most living and progressive, was *baptized into a death*; and endeavoured, by suffering in the flesh, to cease from sin. Of this endeavour, the animating labours and afflictions of early Christianity, the touching asceticism of mediæval Christianity, are the great historical manifestations. Literary monuments of it, each in its own way incomparable, remain in the Epistles of St. Paul, in St. Augustine's *Confessions,* and in the two original and simplest books of the *Imitation.*[1]

Of two disciplines laying their main stress, the one, on clear intelligence, the other, on firm obedience; the one, on comprehensively knowing the grounds of one's duty, the other, on diligently practising it; the one, on taking all possible care (to use Bishop Wilson's words again) that the light we have be not darkness, the other, that according to the best light we have we diligently walk,—the priority naturally belongs to that discipline which braces all man's moral powers, and founds for him an indispensable basis of character. And, therefore, it is justly said of the Jewish people, who were charged with setting powerfully forth that side of the divine order to which the words *conscience* and *self-conquest* point, that they were "entrusted with the oracles of God"; as it is justly said of Christianity, which followed Judaism and which set forth this side with a much deeper effectiveness and a much wider influence, that the wisdom of the old Pagan world was foolishness compared to it. No words of devotion and admiration can

[1] The two first books. (Arnold's note.)

be too strong to render thanks to these beneficent forces which have so borne forward humanity in its appointed work of coming to the knowledge and possession of itself; above all, in those great moments when their action was the wholesomest and the most necessary.

But the evolution of these forces, separately and in themselves, is not the whole evolution of humanity,— their single history is not the whole history of man; whereas their admirers are always apt to make it stand for the whole history. Hebraism and Hellenism are, neither of them, the *law* of human development, as their admirers are prone to make them; they are, each of them, *contributions* to human development,—august contributions, invaluable contributions; and each showing itself to us more august, more invaluable, more preponderant over the other, according to the moment in which we take them, and the relation in which we stand to them. The nations of our modern world, children of that immense and salutary movement which broke up the Pagan world, inevitably stand to Hellenism in a relation which dwarfs it, and to Hebraism in a relation which magnifies it. They are inevitably prone to take Hebraism as the law of human development, and not as simply a contribution to it, however precious. And yet the lesson must perforce be learned, that the human spirit is wider than the most priceless of the forces which bear it onward, and that to the whole development of man Hebraism itself is, like Hellenism, but a contribution.

Perhaps we may help ourselves to see this clearer by an illustration drawn from the treatment of a single great idea which has profoundly engaged the human spirit, and has given it eminent opportunities for showing its nobleness and energy. It surely must be perceived that the idea of immortality, as this idea rises in its generality before the human spirit, is something grander, truer, and more satisfying, than it is in the particular forms by which St. Paul, in the famous fifteenth chapter of the Epistle to the Corinthians, and Plato, in the *Phædo,* endeavour to develop and establish it. Surely we cannot but feel, that the argumentation with which the Hebrew apostle goes about to expound this great idea is, after all, confused and inconclusive; and that the reasoning, drawn from analogies of likeness and equality, which is employed upon it by the Greek philosopher, is over-subtle and sterile. Above and beyond the inadequate solutions which Hebraism and Hellenism here attempt, extends the immense and august problem itself, and the human spirit which gave birth to it. And this single illustration may suggest to us how the same thing happens in other cases also.

But meanwhile, by alternations of Hebraism and Hellenism, of a man's intellectual and moral impulses, of the effort to see things as they really are, and the effort to win peace by self-conquest, the human spirit proceeds; and each of these two forces has its appointed hours of culmination and seasons of rule. As the great movement of Christianity was a triumph of Hebraism and man's moral impulses, so the great movement which goes by the name of the Renascence[1] was an uprising and re-instatement of man's intellectual impulses and of Hellenism. We in England, the devoted children of Protestantism, chiefly know the Renascence by its subordinate and secondary side of the Reformation. The Reformation has been often called a Hebraising revival, a return to the ardour and sincereness of primitive Christianity. No one, however, can study the development of

[1] I have ventured to give to the foreign word *Renaissance,*—destined to become of more common use amongst us as the movement which it denotes comes, as it will come, increasingly to interest us,—an English form. (*Arnold's note.*)

Protestantism and of Protestant churches without feeling that into the Reformation too,—Hebraising child of the Renascence and offspring of its fervour, rather than its intelligence, as it undoubtedly was,—the subtle Hellenic leaven of the Renascence found its way, and that the exact respective parts, in the Reformation, of Hebraism and of Hellenism, are not easy to separate. But what we may with truth say is, that all which Protestantism was to itself clearly conscious of, all which it succeeded in clearly setting forth in words, had the characters of Hebraism rather than of Hellenism. The Reformation was strong, in that it was an earnest return to the Bible and to doing from the heart the will of God as there written. It was weak, in that it never consciously grasped or applied the central idea of the Renascence, —the Hellenic idea of pursuing, in all lines of activity, the law and science, to use Plato's words, of things as they really are. Whatever direct superiority, therefore, Protestantism had over Catholicism was a moral superiority, a superiority arising out of its greater sincerity and earnestness,—at the moment of its apparition at any rate,—in dealing with the heart and conscience. Its pretensions to an intellectual superiority are in general quite illusory. For Hellenism, for the thinking side in man as distinguished from the acting side, the attitude of mind of Protestantism towards the Bible in no respect differs from the attitude of mind of Catholicism towards the Church. The mental habit of him who imagines that Balaam's ass spoke, in no respect differs from the mental habit of him who imagines that a Madonna of wood or stone winked; and the one, who says that God's Church makes him believe what he believes, and the other, who says that God's Word makes him believe what he believes, are for the philosopher perfectly alike in not really and truly knowing, when they say *God's*

Church and *God's Word,* what it is they say, or whereof they affirm.

In the sixteenth century, therefore, Hellenism re-entered the world, and again stood in presence of Hebraism,—a Hebraism renewed and purged. Now, it has not been enough observed, how, in the seventeenth century, a fate befell Hellenism in some respects analogous to that which befell it at the commencement of our era. The Renascence, that great re-awakening of Hellenism, that irresistible return of humanity to nature and to seeing things as they are, which in art, in literature, and in physics, produced such splendid fruits, had, like the anterior Hellenism of the Pagan world, a side of moral weakness and of relaxation or insensibility of the moral fibre, which in Italy showed itself with the most startling plainness, but which in France, England, and other countries was very apparent too. Again this loss of spiritual balance, this exclusive preponderance given to man's perceiving and knowing side, this unnatural defect of his feeling and acting side, provoked a reaction. Let us trace that reaction where it most nearly concerns us.

Science has now made visible to everybody the great and pregnant elements of difference which lie in race, and in how signal a manner they make the genius and history of an Indo-European people vary from those of a Semitic people. Hellenism is of Indo-European growth, Hebraism is of Semitic growth; and we English, a nation of Indo-European stock, seem to belong naturally to the movement of Hellenism. But nothing more strongly marks the essential unity of man, than the affinities we can perceive, in this point or that, between members of one family of peoples and members of another. And no affinity of this kind is more strongly marked than that likeness in the strength and prominence of the moral fibre, which, notwithstanding immense elements of difference, knits in some special sort the genius and history of us English, and our American descendants across the Atlantic, to the genius and history of the Hebrew people. Puritanism, which has been so great a power in the English nation, and in the strongest part of the English nation, was originally the reaction in the seventeenth century of the conscience and moral sense of our race, against the moral indifference and lax rule of conduct which in the sixteenth century came in with the Renascence. It was a reaction of Hebraism against Hellenism; and it powerfully manifested itself, as was natural, in a people with much of what we call a Hebraising turn, with a signal affinity for the bent which was the master-bent of Hebrew life. Eminently Indo-European by its *humour*, by the power it shows, through this gift, of imaginatively acknowledging the multiform aspects of the problem of life, and of thus getting itself unfixed from its own over-certainty, of smiling at its own over-tenacity, our race has yet (and a great part of its strength lies here), in matters of practical life and moral conduct, a strong share of the assuredness, the tenacity, the intensity of the Hebrews. This turn manifested itself in Puritanism, and has had a great part in shaping our history for the last two hundred years. Undoubtedly it checked and changed amongst us that movement of the Renascence which we see producing in the reign of Elizabeth such wonderful fruits. Undoubtedly it stopped the prominent rule and direct development of that order of ideas which we call by the name of Hellenism, and gave the first rank to a different order of ideas. Apparently, too, as we said of the former defeat of Hellenism, if Hellenism was defeated, this shows that Hellenism was imperfect, and that its ascendency at that moment would not have been for the world's good.

Yet there is a very important difference between the defeat inflicted on Hellenism by Christianity eighteen hundred years ago, and the check given to the Renascence by Puritanism. The greatness of the difference is well measured by the difference in force, beauty, significance, and usefulness, between primitive Christianity and Protestantism. Eighteen hundred years ago it was altogether the hour of Hebraism. Primitive Christianity was legitimately and truly the ascendant force in the world at that time, and the way of mankind's progress lay through its full development. Another hour in man's development began in the fifteenth century, and the main road of his progress then lay for a time through Hellenism. Puritanism was no longer the central current of the world's progress, it was a side stream crossing the central current and checking it. The cross and the check may have been necessary and salutary, but that does not do away with the essential difference between the main stream of man's advance and a cross or side stream. For more than two hundred years the main stream of man's advance has moved towards knowing himself and the world, seeing things as they are, spontaneity of consciousness; the main impulse of a great part, and that the strongest part, of our nation has been towards strictness of conscience. They have made the secondary the principal at the wrong moment, and the principal they have at the wrong moment treated as secondary. This contravention of the natural order has produced, as such contravention always must produce, a certain confusion and false movement, of which we are now beginning to feel, in almost every direction, the inconvenience. In all directions our habitual causes of action seem to be losing efficaciousness, credit, and control, both with others and even with ourselves. Everywhere we see the beginnings of confusion, and we want a clue to some sound order and authority. This we can only get by going back upon the actual instincts and forces which rule our life, seeing them as they really are, connecting them with other instincts and forces, and enlarging our whole view and rule of life.